All you need to know about

THE INTERNET

the internet magazine
.net

All you need to know about

THE INTERNET

by Davey Winder

Future Publishing Limited
Beauford Court
30 Monmouth Street
Bath
Avon BA1 2BW

All you need to know about THE INTERNET
Copyright 1994 Future Publishing Limited. All rights reserved. No part of this
publication may be reproduced in any form except as permitted by the Copyright
Designs and Patents Act 1988. Enquiries for permission to reproduce material should
be directed to the publisher.

 **Future Publishing Limited**, Beauford Court, 30 Monmouth
Street, Bath, Avon BA1 2BW

ISBN 1-85870-064-7

British Library Cataloguing in Publication Data
A CIP catalogue record for this book is available from the British Library

Reprinted three times in 1995

Books Editor Ian Jones

Book Design Rod Lawton

Subbing and layout Tim Norris

Cover origination Nick Aspell

Printed and bound by Ashford Colour Press, Gosport, Gwent

Contents

Chapter 3

The UK Service Providers 17

Chapter 4

Making the connection – the Internet basics 27

Chapter 5

Setting up the Chameleon Sampler 31

Chapter 6

Electronic mail – what is it and why use it? 41

Chapter 7

FTP – File Transfer Protocol 63

Chapter 8

Wavey Davey's FTP Site Directory 77

Chapter 9

World Wide Web 85

Chapter 10

Wavey Davey's World Wide Web Directory 97

Chapter 11

Chapter 12

Chapter 13

Chapter 14

Chapter 15

Chapter 21

Wavey Davey's Mad Mailing List Directory

Chapter 22

Accessing the Internet – a hands-on look

Chapter 21

Cyber-Societies

Chapter 24

FAQs

Dedication

For Yvonne, my Ballerina Girl, now and always.

Acknowledgements

There really are so many people involved in getting a book such as this one out of the mind of the author and onto the shelves in the shops, I cannot hope to mention them all here. However, the following people have my special, and heartfelt, thanks for their invaluable assistance:

Ian Jones for commissioning the project and believing in me.
Simon Cooke for being a great friend and helping me whenever I need it.
Karen Gentleman for allowing my ego in her house.
The Clark family for giving birth to such a wonderful daughter.
Nikita and Holly for being everything a Daddy could want.

Finally a very, very big thank you to everyone who has helped me along the way. You all know who you are! The people who inhabit the on-line world make writing a book such as this a pleasure, not a task.

About the author

Davey Winder, also known as "Wavey Davey", is a very well known character in cyberspace. The Observer described him in 1994 as being "one of the UK's first Virtual Celebrities" whilst the BBC introduced him as being "the UK's foremost guide to the Internet". There is even now a Usenet Newsgroup called "alt.fan.wavey.davey" as if his ego wasn't big enough already! As well as writing for many different computer magazines, Davey also appears on television and radio talking about the Internet.

Davey Winder doesn't, however, just write about the Internet. He uses it on a daily basis and has done for many years now. He is gifted with the ability to be able to remain enthusiastic about the subject, without getting bogged down in technicalities, which makes him one of the most readable and interesting authors writing about the Internet today.

Happy to practise what he preaches, Davey will be glad to receive email from any readers of this book .For criticism, technical help, or just a chat, please feel free to contact the author at any of the following addresses (Davey cannot guarantee he will reply, but will do his best to do so. Please allow for the fact that he is a very busy man, and that it may well take a few days for him to find the time to mail you.) which are given in no particular order of preference:

```
dwindera@cix.compulink.co.uk
waveydavey@delphi.com
wavey@dircon.co.uk
davey@wavey.demon.co.uk
74431.1365@compuserve.com
wavey@waveydavey.win-uk.net
davey@ibmpcug.co.uk
```

Other titles by the same author: 'Internet, Modems, and the Whole Comms Thing' – Future Publishing

All you need to know about the Internet

Introduction

I guess you have heard a lot of talk about the Internet recently. It seems you can't switch on your radio or television without someone talking about it. Open your newspaper and the chances are it's mentioned in there somewhere as well. Trendy terminology such as "information super-highway", "global email", "cyberspace", and "netsurfing" fight for your attention. Perhaps you are asking yourself what it all means, what the Internet really is, and how it can be of use to you? Maybe you are wondering just how you go about getting connected?

"All You Need To Know About The Internet" will answer these questions and more, helping you to discover the Internet without hassle or heartache.

And to make it even easier, we've included icons in the margins to draw your attention to especially important pieces of information. Here are the icons, together with an explanation of what they mean (although it's all pretty obvious):

Make a note. Most of the things you read get stored away in your head somewhere or other. When you see this icon, though, make sure you store this particular item somewhere prominent. It's quite important.

Top Tip. There are lots of ways of saving time, money and effort that you'll never see in print. Except here, that is.

What does it mean? Anything to do with the Internet is packed with jargon. You can't get rid of it, you just have to live with it. But that doesn't mean to say you can't explain it...

Warning! You won't see this icon too often, but when you do, pay attention! Ignoring it could cost you time, money or your sanity. And none of us have much to spare of any of those.

Chapter I

The Internet – what the heck is it?

The simplest way to describe the Internet is as a global network of computer networks. The networks that comprise the Internet vary from huge Government departments, university and college networks, large corporates such as IBM, through to commercial on-line systems such as Cix, CompuServe and Delphi, and non-profit making organisations as well. The scale of the thing is quite awesome – more than 30 million people connected to the Internet through something like 3 million computers, statistics that continue to grow on a daily basis. All these people using the resource that is the Internet for a myriad of different purposes, including email, file transfer, information retrieval, social chitchat, even checking on the news and weather!

History of the Net

The Internet was conceived way back in 1969 when the Defense Advanced Research Projects Agency (DARPA), a United States defence department, found a need for a method of exchanging military research information between researchers based at different sites. A network, consisting of just four computers, was established and went by the name of the DARPANET. By 1972 there were 37 computers, or nodes, on the network which had become known by now as ARPANET due to a change in the name of the agency responsible. However, along with the growth of the network had come change – change in the way it was being used. No longer was it just a vehicle for the exchange of research data, now its users were talking to each other through private electronic mailboxes. ARPANET saw a continued and steady growth, and its users continued to diversify. A separate network, MILNET, was created in 1983 to enable the sensitive military research to continue without fear of compromise from the ever growing number of people using ARPANET.

If the Internet was conceived in 1969 then I guess you could say the baby was delivered in 1984 when the National Science Foundation (yet another United States Government Agency) established the NSFNET. The NSF had created five supercomputer centres whose resources were required to be accessible to any educational facility who wanted them. These centres were to give the academic world access to some of the world's fastest computers, and were so expensive that only five could be built!

Originally the plan had been to use ARPANET to allow for the distribution of this information, but this was scuppered largely by red tape. Instead the NSF took matters into their own hands and came up with the NSFNET which used the same basic technology as ARPANET, connecting educational facilities on a regional basis. Each region had at least one site connected directly to a supercomputer centre, and so therefore every site in the region was also connected piggy back style, passing the information along a route of computer sites. NSFNET was remarkably successful. So successful, in fact, that the system was fast becoming overloaded by 1987 with so many people using it, and many of them not for the original purposes of academic research.

In 1987 the NSF network was given a massive overhaul, with faster telephone lines and computers, and opened up to just about any academic researcher, government employee and even international research organisation provided they were from countries who were allies of the United States. Into the 1990s and the network, or the Internet as it was now known officially, was made accessible to anyone who could connect.

Who's using the Internet and why?

The Internet is used by people from all walks of life, not just the scientists, teachers, librarians and computer buffs that you may imagine. There are bikers, businessmen (and women), doctors, lawyers, writers, kids, rock stars, housewives, even the odd MP (aren't they all?) or two. In fact, as the Internet gets more and more media coverage, more and more people are realising the potential there and are getting connected. Don't think for a minute that it is just individuals out there having a friendly natter either, because it isn't. There are ever increasing numbers of businesses who have found that they can offer excellent customer support, make and maintain business contacts, and perform mundane administrative tasks all using the Internet.

For the sake of keeping things simple, let's divide the Internet into five main application groups:

○ Electronic Mail

○ Information Browsing

○ File Transfer

○ Socialising

○ Using Other Computers

Electronic mail

Without doubt the biggest single use of the Internet would have to be electronic mail. Email is so much faster than traditional methods of sending documents, and has the advantage of not just being limited to words. Images, sounds, and indeed whole executable computer programs can be sent across the world, in an instant, using electronic mail. Binary files can be turned into text using a simple program and then sent as email, and with the development of Multi-purpose Internet Mail Extensions (MIME for short) you can now attach binary programs such as spreadsheets and graphics files to your email messages. You can send copies of your mail to any number of people at the same time and you can easily scan the mail in your mailbox to see who has sent what in much less time than it would take to open a doormat full of letters! Email is efficient and convenient, what more could anyone want?

Information browsing

One of the things that computers do very well is search through large databases very quickly locating information that you have asked for by specifying a keyword. Think about the amount of information that can be kept in one database on an average sized PC, quite a bit huh? Now think about how much more information can be stored on a database that runs on a large computer serving a network. And now try to imagine, if you can, the sheer volume of information that is stored on all the computer networks that go up to make the Internet, and then let the realisation dawn upon you that you can actually access an awful lot of those databases from the comfort of your own computer. There are applications such as ARCHIE and GOPHER which make searching and retrieving this information simplicity itself, so easy that even a very silly man who has taken a silly tablet could do it. I know, I was that man.

WHAT
DOES IT
MEAN

ARCHIE lets you find where files that are available for anonymous FTP are kept on the Internet, while GOPHER allows you to wander through many different networks looking for files, databases, documents etc, all from one simple menu and without you even realising you are surfing around the globe.

MAKE A
NOTE!

Even more exciting than Gophers, however, and certainly the current big growth area for Internet use is the World Wide Web. Also known as W3 but the accepted acronym is really WWW, the Web is a hypertext based system that allows you to browse Internet resources.

It is becoming so popular because the most commonly used of the WWW "browser" programs, Mosaic, allows even the most computer and communications illiterate user to painlessly travel through the Web of Net resources, including text, images, and sound (even video is making an appearance). Mosaic turns your computer screen into a World Wide Web interactive magazine, and you can't help but want to turn the page and see what waits around the corner. Turning the page you may well find news, weather, pictures from the hubble space telescope, details of what's on the TV, virtual museums, electronic magazines, the list is almost endless. Heck, I even discovered Elvis on the World Wide Web.

File transfer

The Internet is quite literally littered with files. No matter which side road you may pull into, the chances are you will see files on the sidewalk (sidewalk? This is a UK book, say pavement, man!). These files may be documents, pictures, sounds, or executable programs. The ability to move files around over the Internet is paramount, especially if you are involved in research work or trying to run a business involving product support, upgrades etc. Even if you are using the Net purely for pleasure you will still want to grab interesting files when you come across them. Thankfully this isn't a task fraught with problems, FTP (File Transfer Protocol) allows you to move files with ease. The Internet is probably the worlds biggest shareware library, with programs that suit every conceivable need. Although there are many archive sites that you won't be able to use because you don't have access to them, unless you are a member of that particular organisation or have been granted access privileges, there are even more sites that allow what is know as Anonymous FTP.

Anonymous FTP refers to an archive site that allows anyone to access it, or more usually a public directory held at that site, without having been granted any special access rights. Some of these sites hold vast amount of data, and I mean vast, we are talking Gigabytes here.

Socialising

How could you possibly be part of a world-wide system used by millions of people and not want to talk to some of them? Well quite, you couldn't, could you? Luckily the Internet is very well set up to allow for social interaction. Best loved, and hated at times, is Usenet. This is a system whereby you can participate in discussions on just about any possible subject by subscribing (free of charge) to any number of "newsgroups".

A simple program called a newsreader is required to access Usenet, and allows you to both read and post to the newsgroups.

There are thousands of these groups covering everything from the Internet itself, through space and alien visitors, to Windows and talking like the Swedish chef from the Muppet show (I really don't know why those two seemed to come into my mind at the same time!).

 Similar to Usenet newsgroups, in that they are essentially forums for debate and discussion, are mailing lists.

Postings to a mailing list are made by email to a central site, quite often a host machine called a listserver, and are then distributed (again by email) to all members who have subscribed to that particular list. Subscribing to a list costs nothing, except in some cases a full to overflowing mailbox every day!

 Another form of social contact is the real time conversations that are enabled under Internet Relay Chat or IRC for short. If you think of this as being the hi-tech answer to Citizens Band Radio you won't be far off the truth.

IRC has a reputation, somewhat deserved, for being the home to lots of rather silly students. However, it is possible to find channels where sensible discussion is taking place, and it can be a very stimulating and useful resource on the odd ocassion.

Social contact over the Internet is a very real phenomena, it isn't just sad people talking about the bugs in their compiler. I know of a number of people who have met the girl/boy of their dreams, fallen in love, and in a couple of cases got married after "meeting" this way.

What does the future hold?

Perhaps the biggest strength of the Internet may also be its biggest potential weakness, and that is the staggering rate of growth of the Net. Conservative estimates reckon that this growth is at a rate of somewhere in the region of between 5% and 10% every single month as more and more

All you need to know about the Internet

people and organisations arrive on-line. This could mean that existing resources would have to start slowing up until the Infobahn became the on-line equivalent of the M25. The answer is in ensuring that the infrastructure of the Net expands to support the continued growth. If you think of the network connections as simple pipelines, if more and more people are sending more and more files along the pipes then eventually the pipes are going to get blocked unless someone installs more pipework!

One of the ways that this sort of expansion will happen is by the ever increasing commercialisation of the Internet. Not necessarily as bad a thing as some of the Internet Old Timers would have you believe, in my opinion. What's wrong with an Internet connection being as easy to get installed as a telephone line is? Why not work in cyberspace? I do! Home shopping could become a reality not just the subject of popular television news stories. Remember the future is now, grab hold of it and use it.

Using other computers

No, I'm not talking about hacking here. No, just because you are on the Internet doesn't mean that anyone else also connected can somehow get into the computer on your desk and remove all those top secret files of yours.

MAKE A
NOTE!
Someone cannot magically send a virus to infect your machine without you downloading and running an infected executable program. There, I'm glad we've got that out of the way.

What I am talking about, however, is the fact that you can connect to computers that you have authority to use, via the Internet, and to all intents and purposes let your computer act as if it were another terminal on that system. For example, I belong to an on-line system in San Francisco Bay called The WELL. It would cost me a fortune to call the United States from my home in London to use this system, instead I make a local phone call to my Internet service provider and then use an application called Telnet to connect across the Internet to the WELL system. Once connected this way I can do everything that I could do if I had telephoned them direct, as I am actually connected to their system.

So where do I go from here?

Hopefully the answer to the question raised in the title of this section is "straight into cyberspace". I would imagine you can't wait to get out there and start experiencing the Internet for yourself. Well sit tight for just a little while and read this book first, it could save you from making expensive mistakes along the way.

Remember the best thing to do is look at what you want out of the Internet and then get the right equipment and the right Internet connection to suit your needs. Take a careful look at the sections about service providers, decide if you need a direct connection straight away or if you would be adequately served by using one of the dial up services. Once you have decided which type of connection is best for you, the chances are that the service provider you have chosen will be looked at in some depth in this book, telling you the easy way to connect and giving you a quick guide to getting round their particular system. The information given in this book won't be exhaustive nor comprehensive, but it will be enough for you to be able to get on-line and find out more from there…

When on-line you'll need somewhere to go and something to do. That's where the reference sections of the book come in, with roadmaps for your journey down the information superhighway in the form of resource directories. These list all types of services, giving exactly the details you will need to be able to connect to them without hassle. If you are new to comms then make sure you keep a copy of this book on your desk, the glossary, smiley dictionary, and acronym dictionary should help you make sense of some of the apparent nonsense you might discover along the way.

Above all else, have fun, be productive, and take a drive into the future.

Chapter 2

Getting connected

Connecting to the Internet is easy these days, providing you follow some basic guidelines which we'll look at in a moment. First though, just what do you need to start your journey into cyberspace?

Internet connection checklist

○ A computer

○ A modem

○ A telephone line

○ Communications software

○ Internet Service Provider

To cut through all the cack, in the simplest terms you just connect the modem to the computer, plug the modem into the telephone line, run your software, and let the system call your service provider. Hey presto, you are on the Net! Now let's take a slightly more in depth look at what you need...

The computer

You don't have to have the most powerful computer in the world to connect to the most powerful computer network. One of the wonderful things about the Internet is that it is all about communication, and that communication doesn't rely on any one hardware platform.

MAKE A
NOTE!

You can connect to the Net using an Amiga, Atari ST, Archimedes, Macintosh or PC. In fact, whatever computer you happen to use will be able to get you connected to the Internet. Of course, the more powerful your computer the more powerful Internet access software you will be able to run on it.

My advice is to use the computer you are happy with – chances are you already use a particular platform so why change just to use the Internet? If you are buying a computer in order to connect to the Net, then look around and see which system you are happiest using. You should consider a machine that has a hard disk – although you can use the Internet without one it is a lot easier to have one, believe me. Similarly you should think about the fastest processor you can afford – a fast machine will be able to handle faster file transfers with less hassle than a slower machine. Make sure that the display is good and clear because low resolution and interlaced displays soon become very tiring on your eyes.

MAKE A
NOTE!

In this book I'll be using a well specified PC running Windows, for the simple reason that there is a lot of very easy to use software available for this particular platform and it is a platform that many people will be familiar with.

What is a modem anyway?

A modem, or MOdulator/DEModulator, is just a device that converts computer data into sound so it can be transmitted across an ordinary telephone line. Computers speak in a language known as binary which is comprised of 0s and 1s, or yeses and nos if you prefer. This digital information cannot be transferred over a telephone line so has to be converted to an analogue signal (in this case sound) first. Your modem handles this conversion, and the modem at the other end of the connection converts this analogue signal back into binary so the computer at that end can understand it. I know it may sound awfully complicated, and that's because it is! But don't panic, all you need to know is that modems work, that's what they are paid for so let them do the worrying.

There are so many modems on the market nowadays that you may think it is almost impossible to make an informed choice. You'd be wrong, so let me help you cut the number down to the range that will suit your needs.

All you need to know about the Internet **.net**

First of all, you need to decide if you want an internal or external modem. Both have advantages and disadvantages. The most obvious advantage of an internal modem is that it doesn't take up any space on your already cluttered desk (well it will be cluttered if it's anything like my desk!). It also leaves the serial port free. However, while this is true you should also think of the disadvantages, such as the fact that the modem will fill an expansion slot in your computer; there won't be front panel status lights to help you trace connection problems; and you can't swap the modem between computer platforms. I prefer to use external modems for these reasons, and would recommend them to you as well especially if you are just getting started in comms.

Next thing to look at is the speed of the modem, and my tip would be to go for the fastest you can possibly afford. The reasoning behind this is simple, the quicker you can transfer information between the Internet and your computer, the less time you will spend connected to the telephone and your service provider. So although you will pay more at the outset for a fast modem you will recoup this, and then some, by the savings in on-line costs.

And talking of saving costs, while modems that are advertised as being Non-BABT approved are usually much cheaper than their approved counterparts, it is illegal to connect them to the telephone system in the UK. BABT approval covers such areas as safety by ensuring that high voltages don't appear on the line as well as usage factors like interference with other telephone users.

Although many people do use unapproved equipment, including telephones and fax machines, you could face disconnection if caught as well as being liable for the cost of any damage and necessary repair caused to the telephone system (including other users equipment) if your unapproved modem is to blame.

Watch out for modems that feature error checking and data compression, as these can dramatically improve performance. The thing to look for is V.42bis, if your modem has this then you will be smokin'...

Communications software

With the explosion in the growth of the Internet has come a comparative explosion in the amount of software available to make accessing it easier. Every computer platform has software that is capable of letting you use the Internet, some of it is good and some of it is quite amazing! You don't have to have communications software with loads of bells and whistles to get onto the Internet, something as simple as the Windows "Terminal" will do the job. However, if you are going to be spending any time connected to the Net, and certainly if you want your time to be as productive as possible, then software which provides the extra tools for the job will be appreciated. A basic minimum requirement would be a program that can handle Xmodem transfers, and either VT100 or VT102 terminal emulation.

If you have just purchased a modem then the chances are that it will have been packaged complete with some communications software, as such bundles are very commonplace. If not then don't panic as you'll find it pretty easy to get hold of from either a shareware library, or your local dealer in the case of commercial software. You will also find some very good Internet specific software accompanying this book.

A program like Smartcom from Hayes will make your on-line life more rewarding.

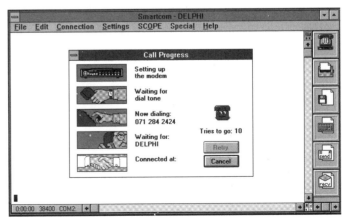

Modem speeds explained

Just what do all those "V" numbers mean? Well they are international standards that have been set by the International Telecommunications Union - Telecommunications (usually referred to as the ITU-T). Although a "V" number usually refers to a modem's speed, this isn't always the case as you can see from this simple guide:

V.21	=	speed of 300 bits per second
V.22	=	speed of 1200 bits per second
V.22bis	=	speed of 2400 bits per second
V.23	=	speed of 1200 bits per second receiving data, and 75 bits per second sending data
V.32	=	speed of 9600 bits per second
V.32bis	=	speed of 14400 bits per second
V.34	=	speed of 28800 bits per second
V.42	=	an error correction standard
V.42bis	=	V.42 error correction combined with data compression

Chapter 3

The UK Service Providers

The Internet service provider is just about the most important link in the chain, for without it you won't get far on your journey down the infobahn. To make any use of the Internet you need to have some form of connection to the network. At it's simplest this may be a Bulletin Board Service which offers an Internet email service by forwarding your mail to a service provider which has an email gateway, at its most complex (and expensive) would be a direct, permanent connection. A service provider, generally a commercial concern, can come in many flavours, but can be broken down into four basic types.

1) Direct or Dedicated Connection

This is a permanent and direct line to the Internet, usually found in Universities, Government Departments (US), and big business. If you don't have access to this type of system, don't even bother thinking about getting one unless you have a lot of spare cash floating around. A dedicated Internet connection can cost many thousands of pounds to set up and maintain. Definitely only for the bigwigs.

2) Dial-In or SLIP/PPP Connection

Perhaps the most common type of Internet connection is that which is offered by a service provider who has a dedicated connection himself, and allows subscribers to telephone in and use that line.

The protocols that make this possible are called SLIP and PPP (PPP is gradually taking over from SLIP) and so the connection is often referred to by these names.

The service provider gives you a host domain of your own, and it is as good as being directly connected yourself. You can do just about everything you could if you had a dedicated line but at a fraction of the cost, for example any files you download are transferred directly to your computer not to the service provider's.

The biggest advantages of using this sort of service provider are that first you get your own domain name rather than being stuck with your host computer's domain name. For example, using the Dial-Up service Delphi

(don't worry, Dial-Up connections will be revealed in just a moment) my
email address is `waveydavey@delphi.com` whereas using the Dial-In
service at Demon Internet I have my own domain of
`[user]@wavey.demon.co.uk` the [user] part can be any name I want,
and as many as I want for email purposes. This feature is pretty useful if you
want to keep email sorted separately, say one email address for business and
another for personal use. Another advantage, becoming ever more
important, is that this sort of connection gives you what you need to be
able to run a graphical World Wide Web browser such as Mosaic. Finally,
you can choose what software you wish to run rather than having to use
whatever the host computer system provides.

On the downside, the software provided by Dial-In services has sometimes
been damn difficult to get set up. However, fear not as the disk included
with the book gives you one of the easiest to use access software suites,
with full step by step instructions in these pages on how to set it all up and
get going.

3) Dial-Up or Terminal Connection

This type of connection is generally provided by the large commercial on-
line systems such as Cix or Delphi in the UK. You subscribe to their system,
which provides much more than just Internet access, and this allows you to
access their Internet Gateway. You stay in "terminal" mode, which means
that your computer isn't seen as being connected to the Internet by other
users, it is the system you have called that is connected and you just have a
terminal that you are using on that host computer. So transferring files, for
example, is a two stage operation. You first have to download them to the
host computer and from there to your computer. Also you cannot use the
graphical World Wide Web browsers with this type of connection, although
most services do have a character based alternative so you can still access
the Web.

The big advantage is that there is no setting up of hardware and software
involved, this is already taken care of at the host system's end. This may also
be noted as a disadvantage of course, as you cannot choose the software
that you like best! The host system may also have set up easy to access

menus (like on Delphi) or have an Off Line Reader to provide a cheap
method of performing common Internet applications (like Ameol on Cix).

4) Mail Only Connection

There are quite a large number of Bulletin Board Services, including many of
the larger commercial BBSs, who now offer an Internet Mail service. This
connection provides a link for sending and receiving email only, nothing
else. While it is quite possible to perform many tasks on the Internet using
email, like file transfers using ftpmail and archie searches for finding files, it
is a bit like eating soup with chopsticks, possible but not the easiest thing in
the world. I'll tell you how to do this later in the book, but unless you are
even more skint than Mr Skint the skint bloke I'd suggest you think about
getting yourself properly connected! One exception being WinNET UK
which provides both Internet email and Usenet News in a very nice out of
the box package.

It doesn't matter which of these types of connection you have, I'll cover
them all in the book. Types 1 and 2 are, for all practical purposes, the same
and will be covered in depth throughout the following chapters. The Dial-
Up services differ quite markedly in how you use them, so I will devote a
chapter on how to use the Internet Gateways on the most popular of these,
including Cix, Delphi, and CompuServe.

UK Internet service providers directory

Your access to the Internet is by means of an "Internet Service Provider" of
one sort or another. There are many different service providers in the UK,
with more appearing at an alarmingly increasing rate (I say 'alarmingly' as I
doubt that they can all survive in such a competitive marketplace as that of
UK Internet provision). Not that you would know this, of course, if you have
been reading any of the dozens of Internet books that have been available
so far, all of which cover the United States in some depth but don't touch
upon the UK.

Well all that has changed, this book is for UK Internet users, and here
follows a fairly comprehensive list of the main players in the UK Internet

service provision stakes as I write. There will, undoubtedly, be more companies offering such services by the time this book actually gets published, but such is life. This little lot have a proven track record and will certainly enable you to get Internet connected with the minimum of fuss. Have a look at what is available, read the whole of this book, get in touch with the various companies, and then decide. The choice is, ultimately, yours. Make it wisely!

Name	**BBC Networking Club**
	PO Box 7
	Broadcasting Support Services
	London W3 6XY
Contact	Phone 081 576 7799
	Fax 081 993 6281
	Email **info@bbcnc.org.uk**
Charges	PC/Mac £25.00 setup and then £12.00 per month.
	Acorn £35.00 setup and then £12.00 per month.
Comments	The BBC are one of the new organisations to join the Internet service provision market. The service provides customised front end software for PC, Macintosh, and Acorn platforms but not, surprisingly, the Amiga. The BBCNC has its own bulletin board called "Auntie" and some very healthy World Wide Web pages.
Name	**CityScape Internet Services Ltd**
	59 Wycliffe Road
	Cambridge
	CB1 3JE
Contact	Phone 0223 566950
	Fax 0223 566951
	Email **sales@cityscape.co.uk**
Charges	Setup fee of £50, and annual charge of £180.
Comments	CityScape have got together with Pipex to provide the IP-Gold service. This provides an easy to install and easy to use "one disk" solution to Internet connectivity for Windows users. Full access to all Internet provisions, with commercial email software, Mail-It, included in the membership cost.

All you need to know about the Internet .net

Name	**Compulink Information eXchange (Cix)**
	The Sanctuary
	Oakhill Grove
	Surbiton
	Surrey KT6 6DU
Contact	Phone 081 390 8446
	Fax 081 390 6561
	Email **cixadmin@cix.compulink.co.uk**
Charges	One time registration fee of £25.00.
	Monthly minimum charge of £6.25 billed in advance and based upon hourly on-line charges of:
	£3.20 peak time (Mon to Fri 8.00am to 5.00pm).
	£2.40 at all other times.
	There are no extra charges for Internet access, over and above the normal on-line charges.
Comments	Cix has a direct connection to the Internet, providing Usenet News, Internet Mail, FTP, Telnet, Gopher, IRC, Archie, Finger and so on. In addition Cix is also the largest conferencing system in the UK, offering full conferencing facilities, over 50 Gigabytes of on-line file storage, and Electronic Mail.

Name	**Delphi Internet**
	The Elephant House
	Hawley Crescent
	London NW1 8NP
Contact	Phone 071 757 7150
	Fax 071 757 7160
	Email **uk@delphi.com**
Charges	There are two payment plans:
	10/4 Plan which costs £10 per month, giving the first four hours of usage free each month, with further hours costing £4 each.
	20/20 Plan which costs £20 per month, giving the first twenty hours of usage free each month, with further hours costing £1.80 each.
	Delphi UK also have a "five free hours" offer which allows

you to look around the system for five hours, free, while you decide if you want to join. The five hours are only valid in the month you take up the offer, and any further hours that month are charged at a rate of £1.80 each.

Comments Delphi UK has a direct dial-up connection to the Internet, providing Usenet news, FTP, Email, Gopher, Telnet, WWW and everything else you would expect. In addition, Delphi UK offers on-line news, forums, databases, full access to the US Delphi system (with more than 100,000 members), and even the chance to win £1000 every month in their Treasure Hunt competition.

Name **Demon Internet Limited**
42 Hendon Lane
London N3 1TT

Contact Phone 081 349 0063 (London)
031 552 0344 (Scotland)
Fax 081 349 0309
Email `internet@demon.net`

Charges There are various charges, depending on the service type you want.
The standard dial-up service has a one off registration fee of £12.50 plus a monthly charge of £10.00.
Mail forwarding is available for a supplement of £200 per year.
The network dial-up, with reserved line, carries an initial fee of £750 plus a monthly charge of £100.
A 14.4K leased line costs an initial £1000 plus a monthly charge of £200.
A 64K leased line is an initial £1000 plus a monthly charge of £400.
There are no on-line time charges, over and above the monthly fee.

Comments Demon Internet offers your own Internet site and address, Electronic Mail directly to and from your site, full access to the Internet, Usenet News. SLIP or PPP dial-in access, network connectivity, and bi-directional and leased lines.

All you need to know about the Internet **.net**

You can have multiple mail addresses, ftp directly to your desktop, all for a standard monthly fee no matter how much you use the service.

Name	**The Direct Connection**
Contact	Phone 081 317 0100 (voice)
	081 317 2222 (modem. use login of "demo")
	Email **helpdesk@dircon.co.uk**
Charges	There are various charges, depending on the service type you want. All are subject to a standard one off registration fee of £7.50.
	Standard login account costs £10.00 per month.
	Enhanced login account costs £20.00 per month.
	TCP/IP account costs £10.00 per month with no extra on-line time charges.
Comments	The Direct Connection has a direct connection to the Internet (no surprises there, huh folks!). It offers networked electronic mail, Usenet News, Telnet, FTP, Archie, Computer Newswire, File areas, IRC, Gopher, World Wide Web, and Fax. Provides excellent technical support, and is one of the longer established service providers in the UK.

Name	**EUnet GB**
	Kent R+D Business Centre
	Giles Lane
	Canterbury
	Kent CT2 7PB
Contact	Phone 0227 266466
Charges	There are various charges, depending on the service type you want.
	Contact EUnet for details.
Comments	EUnet GB was formerly known as UKnet, and has been providing Internet services in the UK since 1982. Full IP services were introduced in 1991, and now EUnet can offer services ranging from a world-wide email system to full leased line Internet connectivity with router.

Name	**ExNet**
Contact	Phone "Freephone" Internet or 081 244 0077
	Email **exnet@exnet.com**
Charges	From £87 per year.
Comments	ExNet was only just arriving on the scene when I wrote this book, so I don't know that much about them yet! They provide a full Internet connection at a reasonable price.

Name	**PC User Group**
Contact	Phone 081 863 1191
	Email **info@ibmpcug.co.uk**
Charges	There are various charges, depending on the type of service you want and whether you are a member of the PC User Group or not. WinNet account costs from £6.75 per month. Interactive Premium Service account costs an extra £7.25 per month.
Comments	The PC User Group offers a service that includes a BBS, Usenet News, UUCP, electronic mail, and Internet access. They also provide WinNET which is a very easy to use email and Usenet News "off line reader" for Windows users.

Name	**Pipex Ltd** 216 Cambridge Science Park Milton Road Cambridge CB4 4WA
Contact	Phone 0223 250120 Fax 0223 250121 Email **pipex@pipex.net**
Charges	There are numerous different charges depending on the type of service option. Not all variations are mentioned here as it would take too long to list them all! Contact Pipex for details. **Pipex Solo** Set up fee of £50, and an annual fee of £180 (payable quarterly in advance).

All you need to know about the Internet **.net**

Comments   Pipex offers commercial Internet access via a range of dial-in
                 and leased line services. The Pipex Solo service is, essentially,
                 the same thing as CityScape IP-Gold, but for existing Pipex
                 corporate customers only. Pipex is the Public IP Exchange,
                 part of the Unipalm Group, and the UK's leading
                 commercial Internet provider.

Chapter 4

Making the connection –

the Internet basics

There are a few basic things that you need to know about connecting to the Internet right at the start, an understanding of them will help when it comes to getting connected for the first time.

Protocols

You will hear mention of protocols all the time in relation to the Internet, and that is because they are very important things. Protocols are simply the methods that computers use to communicate with each other. The ones that you are likely to be confronted with are as follows:

FTP   File Transfer Protocol. This is what is used to move files between Internet machines. If someone says you can "ftp a file from ...." they are telling you where you can find a file to download to your computer.

POP   Post Office Protocol. Used to transfer email between Internet hosts, and starting to take over from the long established SMTP protocol.

PPP   Point to Point Protocol. This allows a computer to use the Internet with a standard telephone line and modem, rather than having a dedicated Internet connection.

SLIP   Serial Line Internet Protocol. Serves the same function as PPP, but is an older protocol and is much more widely used presently.

SMTP   Simple Mail Transfer Protocol. Used to transfer email between hosts, now starting to get replaced by POP as the email protocol of choice.

TCP/IP   Transmission Control Protocol/Internet Protocol. These are the underlying protocols on which the Internet runs, you will hear them mentioned wherever anoraks get together.

Hosts

A host is a machine (it may be a computer or network of computers) that is attached to, and part of, the Internet. A host has an Internet address, usually referred to as a hostname although there is also an "IP" address which is numerical. In fact, what most people refer to as a hostname is in reality a domain name, the host forming part of the name. As an example let's look at an email address of `teapot@wavey.demon.co.uk`

These addresses should be read from right to left, just to be awkward, so starting at the far right you have the country where the host is located (uk), then comes the type of organisation which in this case is a commercial one (co), to the left of that is the name of the site that provides the service (demon) and finally my host name at the Demon site (Wavey). Anything before the "@" symbol refers to an individual user at that domain or host. For a closer look at domain names and an explanation of all the various codes that can be used refer to the chapter on electronic mail.

The IP address, that's the numerical version of the hostname, consists of four numbers, each less than 256, separated by periods. You don't have to remember these numbers, thankfully, as the hostname will automatically get resolved into the IP number. An example of an IP address is `193.128.225.153` which is also `davey@dircon.co.uk`

Logins and passwords

When you register with your service provider, whichever type it may be, you will need a login or username. Choose this carefully as you may not be able to change it easily later. You may think that a username of "cyberlord" or "fluffybottom" is a pretty good idea, but will you be taken seriously with a name like that? What if you want to conduct business dealings, maybe a more sensible name would be better? Similarly if you just want to be a Net Surfer and use your account to generally hang around the street corners of the Internet, then `jsmith001` isn't the way cool approach. And now I bet I get email from `jsmith001@somewhere.in.cyberspace` complaining bitterly that he isn't a duffle coat donning doughnut head!

You will also have to choose a password so that nobody else can use your account. Passwords are generally restricted to eight letters or less, and you will usually be allocated one when you first sign up with your service provider. You should change this password to one of your own the first time you use the account.

Don't choose passwords that are easy to guess. Things like the name of your kids or pet rabbit are a no-no, as are your nickname and words such as "password" "secure" and "knob".

The best passwords are those comprising a random jumble of characters, for example BoB%$9m. Of course, the problem is then remembering it without resorting to sticking a Post-It note on your computer! An easier method is to mix a random word such as "noddy" with random characters to become a password of no!dd$Y

For added peace of mind, change your password regularly. Oh, and don't panic if you forget your password. Just contact your service provider and they will supply you with a new one so you can get connected and change it to something else again!

Chapter 5

Setting up the Chameleon Sampler

On the disk that comes with this book you will find the Chameleon
Sampler from NetManage. Chameleon is a suite of integrated
programs running under Windows, and lets you get the very best out of the
Internet. The sampler is a cut down version of this suite which includes FTP,
Mail, Telnet and Ping as well as the main custom program to make your
connection. For details of the full Chameleon program and details of how to
purchase this at a special price check out the offer at the back of the book.

Before you can use the Chameleon software included on the disk, you will
need to get yourself an account with a service provider. Chameleon will
only work if you have a Dial-In SLIP/PPP connection to the Internet, of the
type provided by such concerns as Demon Internet and The Direct
Connection. In the following examples in getting set up and connected
with Chameleon I have used The Direct Connection as the service provider,
however it doesn't matter if you are using a different provider as the
principles are the same.

Ensure that you have the full details of your Internet account before you
attempt to install Chameleon. You will require the following information:

• **Login name**
• **Password**
• **Service provider telephone number**
• **Access type**
• **IP address**
• **Host name**
• **Domain name**
• **Domain server**
• **Mail gateway**

All this information should be supplied by your service provider when you
set up an account with them.

Installing the Chameleon sampler

1: Run Windows

2: Insert the disk into your floppy drive

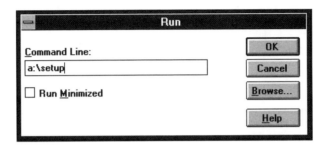

3: Click on the file menu and select "run". In the command line box enter the following (assuming that your floppy drive is A: and your hard drive is C:) and press return

a:\setup

Chameleon will now install itself onto your hard drive. When completed press "OK" and then reboot your computer. You should now have a Chameleon Sampler program group.

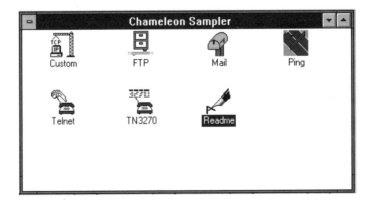

Setting up Chameleon

Please note that entries shown in this example are for my account with The Direct Connection and won't work for you. You must enter the details given by your service provider which relate to your account.

1: Select the Chameleon Sampler program group.

2: Select the "custom" icon.

3: Select the "Interface" menu and then "add"

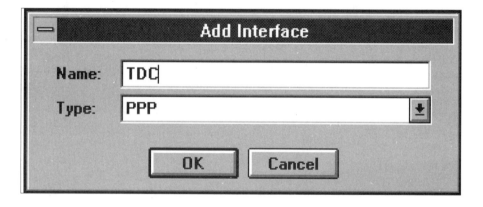

4: In the "Name" field enter the name of your service provider, in this case "TDC".

5: In the "Type" field select either PPP or SLIP according to the details supplied with your Internet account.

6: Select the "Setup" menu and then work your way through all the options as follows.

7: IP Address: for example **193.128.225.1**

8: Subnet Mask: Subnet Value: for example 255.255.255.0
Number of Subnet Mask bits: 0

9: Host Name: This should be the name you have chosen for your system, and is usually the same as your login name. In my example I would enter "wavey"

10: Domain Name: The name of your domain as supplied by the service provider, in this example "`dircon.co.uk`"

11: Port:

Baud Rate: The fastest speed supported by your modem. (The Chameleon Sampler is limited to a maximum speed of 19,200 whereas the full program has a maximum speed of 115,000)

Data Bits: 8

Stop Bits: 1

Parity: None

Connector: The COM port number you are using

Flow Control: Hardware

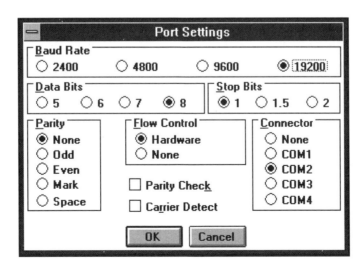

12: Modem: If your modem isn't supported here then select "Hayes". Check your modem documentation for what the default strings should be.

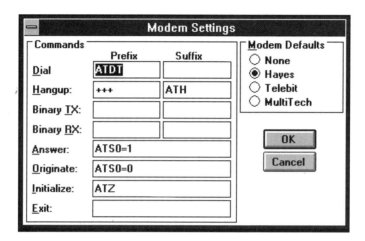

13: Dial: The number of the service provider.

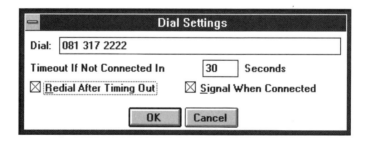

14: Login Settings:

User Name: Enter your login ID, for example wavey
User Password: Your password
Startup Command: Leave this blank

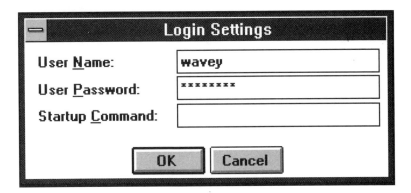

15: Select the "Services" menu and complete the following options

16: Domain Servers: As given by your provider. In this example
193.128.224.1

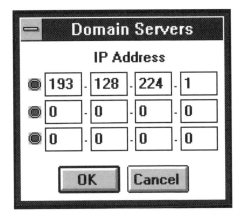

17: Default Gateway: As given by your provider. In this example 193.128.225.1 but don't worry if you cannot select this option due to it being shaded out.

18: Host Table: Leave this blank

19: Save your file by using the "Save As" option from the File menu.

You should now, assuming everything has been set up correctly, be able to connect to your service provider. To test this out, select "Connect" and you should hear your modem start dialling. Once a connection has been made the name displayed in the lower part of the custom window should change from TDC to +TDC.

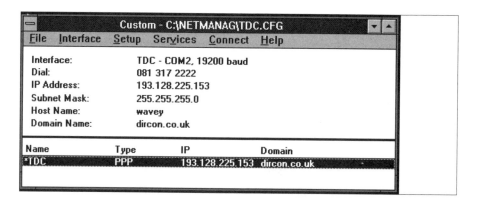

Leave the custom window open, otherwise Chameleon will disconnect from your service provider. Now start the "Ping" program by clicking on its icon in the Chameleon Sampler program group. Select "Start" and enter the IP address of your provider in the "Host" box. Using The Direct Connection as our example enter the IP address of **193.128.225.1** and select OK. If the connection is working OK this should return a result of "1 transmitted 1 received 0% loss". Repeat this using the hostname of your provider, for example "**tdc.dircon.co.uk**" to test that you can resolve IP names to addresses OK. If you get a result of "Failed to resolve host" ensure that you have entered the correct address in the domain servers section of custom. Finally, check that you can communicate with the world at large by entering

an external Internet address such as "**delphi.com**" or
"**cix.compulink.co.uk**".

Congratulations, you are now have an Internet connection! It wasn't that
painful, was it? Now let's take a closer look at how to go about using it!

The ins and outs of the Internet

Or put another way, making the Information Superhighway work for you! In
this section of the book we will look at exactly what you can do once you
are Internet connected, covering everything from email to the World Wide
Web (and lots in between). All in depth, all in an easy to understand way, all
with step by step guides where necessary. I'm not only going to tempt you
with the delights that are on offer, I'm going to give you the recipe to bake
the cake yourself! Before this starts to sound too much like Floyd on
Cyberspace, let's get on with it...

Chapter 6

Electronic mail – what is it and why use it?

Email is the foundation stone upon which the Internet stands and it is the the Internet's most widely used application. Electronic mail refers to messages sent using a computer network as opposed to the traditional methods of pen and paper (which has become widely known to the on-line community as "Snail Mail" due to its comparative slowness!). An email message doesn't have to consist of just text either, oh no. You could send images and sound as well, or maybe a complete piece of software! We'll look at this aspect of electronic mail in more depth in just a moment, but first let's ask the question "why use email?".

OK Postman Pat pickers, here are Wavey's top 5 reasons for using email:

○ Woosh! Email is very fast. Quite often a message sent from the UK can be sitting in a mailbox in Japan within a minute or two, yes that quick. I've known of email that I've sent from London to arrive in the United States in less than 20 seconds, remarkable isn't it?

○ Money! Assuming you have the equipment already, then email is incredibly good value for money. To put it in perspective, sending an urgent letter via the Internet to someone in Tokyo would almost certainly be just a fraction of the cost of making an International telephone call, sending a fax, or sending a letter by recorded delivery.

○ Safe. Yes, I am saying that email is secure (and I dare say that an angry group of duffle coat wearing bowl-heads are rushing to my door this very instant to tell me just how mistaken I must be). Although there have always been doubts about the security of email, which is fair enough as the message might have to travel through a number of computer systems to arrive at its destination, with the arrival of easy to use data encryption programs there is no reason why anyone should be able to read your email even if they wanted to try. You could, of course, send snail mail messages in code if you really wanted to take the time to do it, but a computer is very good at crunching numbers quickly, efficiently, and above all else easily.

○ Efficient. I've already mentioned the obvious advantage of speed, but there are also other aspects of efficiency to look at. For example, it doesn't matter if anyone is in when the mail arrives. It will land in their mailbox and is there to be read the very next time they use their account. Or how about the ease of sending a courtesy copy of your letter to someone else? No need to take a photocopy just tell your mail program to send a copy on. The same applies to forwarding email you get to someone else you may think would be interested – no retyping or photocopying. And if you think of the international angle, with email you don't worry about international time zones or foreign speaking operators as you would with a telephone call.

○ Hi-Tech. Hell yes, why not make use of the technology that is available? With email you can send a message which incorporates a spreadsheet file ready to import into your business colleague's program, or some fancy graphics or a sound sample. If you are a software company you could send upgrades to your programs, complete working executable files, attached to your email.

 Hey, want to complain about a BBC TV programme in a really cool way? Then write to Points Of View by sending Email to:

pov@bbcnc.org.uk
_____

Well that takes care of the *what* and *why*, I guess a good writer would look at the *how* next. So let's look at how then!

Email addresses

Just like traditional "snail mail" depends on the letter being correctly addressed for it to be delivered properly, so does electronic mail. It's no good sending an email message addressed to **waveydavey@internet** and expecting it get to me, it won't!

See just how easy
it is to Email
someone!

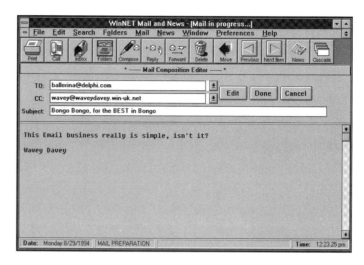

An Internet email address consists of two parts, separated by an @ sign. Anything before the @ separator is the users name, and everything after it is known as the domain. It is easy to understand this concept if you relate it to physical addresses in the "real" world. To post me a bundle of used fivers in a jiffy bag you would have to address the letter to:

Davey Winder, 46b Internet Avenue, Cybertown, UK.

(OK, you got me, that isn't my real address)

If you were to put the @ separator after my name but before the rest you would have something very similar to an email address. Let's look at one a bit closer, using a real address of mine as an example, and do please feel free to send me some mail to try it out!

davey@wavey.demon.co.uk

It is easiest to break down this address by reading it from right to left, so that is what we shall do.

At the far right is what is known as the top level domain, and this can be either the type of organisation, or more commonly the country code. Generally speaking, email addresses that originate from the United

States are less likely to bear a country code. In my address you can see that the top level domain is quite obviously the United Kingdom, however other country codes are not always as obvious. Interestingly enough the official country code for the United Kingdom is actually gb, but uk gets used far more often. In fact I can't remember ever seeing an address with a gb suffix in all my years on the Net!

Next to the top level domain comes the part of the address which tells others my house number, street, and county. In Internet terms this means the computer, site, and service type. Reading from the right, "co" refers to the fact that I'm using a commercial service, "demon" is the name of site that provides my service (Demon Internet), and "wavey" is my hostname at the Demon site.

So you can now send mail to my electronic house if you like, but you still haven't said who the letter is for. This is where you need the username part of the address, the bit that goes before the @ sign. At the example address you would use "wavey" as the username. However, there might be more than one mailbox at the `wavey.demon.co.uk` address so you could send mail to `teapot@wavey.demon.co.uk` if such a user existed. If you are not sure of the username then you can always send mail addressed to postmaster at the site, asking the postmaster to let you know the correct username. For example `postmaster@wavey.demon.co.uk`

Top level domain country codes

Code	Country
aq	Antarctica
ar	Argentina
at	Austria
au	Australia
be	Belgium
br	Brazil
ca	Canada
ch	Switzerland

cl	Chile
cr	Costa Rica
cs	Czechoslovakia
cy	Cyprus
de	Germany
dk	Denmark
ec	Ecuador
ee	Estonia
es	Spain
fi	Finland
fr	France
gl	Greenland
gr	Greece
hk	Hong Kong
hr	Croatia
hu	Hungary
ie	Ireland
il	Israel
in	India
is	Iceland
it	Italy
jp	Japan
kr	Korea (Republic of)
kw	Kuwait
lu	Luxembourg
lv	Latvia
mx	Mexico
my	Malaysia
nt	Netherlands
no	Norway
nz	New Zealand
pl	Poland
pr	Puerto Rico
pt	Portugal
ru	Russian Federation
se	Sweden
sg	Singapore

sk	Slovakia
sl	Slovenia
th	Thailand
tn	Tunisia
tr	Turkey
tw	Taiwan
uk	United Kingdom
us	United States
ve	Venezuela
za	South Africa

Top level domain organisation codes

com	Commercial organisation
edu	Educational facility
gov	Non military government bodies
mil	Military concerns
org	Other organisations
net	Network resources

On your head be it

Although many mail systems allow you to hide email headers, they can be very useful things indeed. A header contains lots of information about the mail, from such obvious things as who sent it, how it was sent, the route it took to get to you, anyone else it was cc'd to, the date it was sent, even who you should reply to if it is someone different from the sender.

If your email doesn't reach its destination, which is known as "bouncing", then the header of the delivery failure message can give you vital clues as to what went wrong.

However, for the most part you can quite safely let your mail program hide the header and just get on with the task of reading the message!

All you need to know about the Internet

A typical Email header, not as complicated as it looks, honest injuns.

```
From wavey@dircon.co.uk  Thu Aug 18 10:57:00 1994
Received: from felix.dircon.co.uk (felix.dircon.co.uk [193.128.224.10]) by cix.compulink.co.uk (8.6.9/8.6.9)
Received: from wavey.dircon.co.uk by felix.dircon.co.uk with SMTP id AA24227
  (5.67b/IDA-1.5); Thu, 18 Aug 1994 10:56:14 +0100
Date: Thu, 18 Aug 94 10:55:05 PDT
Subject: A Message From Elvis
To: wavey@waveydavey.win-uk.net
Cc: dwindera@cix.compulink.co.uk, waveydavey@delphi.com,
     envision@cix.compulink.co.uk
X-Mailer: Chameleon - TCP/IP for Windows by NetManage, Inc.
Message-Id: <Chameleon.4.01.940818105811.Postmaster@>
Mime-Version: 1.0
Content-Type: TEXT/PLAIN; charset=US-ASCII
From: wavey@dircon.co.uk
Apparently-To: dwindera@cix.compulink.co.uk
```

There are lots and lots of famous people using email these days. Feel free to send them email but don't expect an answer, after all most of them are very busy people indeed! Here are just a few well connected people:

Douglas Adams	adamsd@cerf.net
Paddy Ashdown	paddyashdown@cix.compulink.co.uk
Bill Clinton	president@whitehouse.gov
Bill Gates	billg@microsoft.com
Billy Idol	idol@well.sf.ca.us
Terry Pratchett	tpratchett@cix.compulink.co.uk
Bruce Sterling	bruces@well.sf.ca.us

A useful novelty act, code and mime

For a long time now it has been possible to send binary code – that's images, sound, and executable programs – by email. This has been accomplished by converting the binary code to text using a method known as UUencoding and UUdecoding. A simple utility program makes this fairly easy, and as long as the person who receives the mail has the program as well they can decode it and covert the text back into binary. There are limitations to this, however, mainly due to the fact that to safely ensure that the network or mail system doesn't refuse to accept the mail it needs to be sent in fairly small chunks. This involves breaking a large binary file down into a dozen or so pieces of coded email. Although some email systems will automatically piece these segments together and decode them on receipt, the vast majority won't and it is a tiresome and boring task, believe me.

A much better solution to sending binary objects within email is called Multi-purpose Internet Mail Extensions (or MIME for short). A relatively new concept, MIME is set to become the standard method of performing this task.

MIME is a specification for sending files attached to email messages, and as such it really shouldn't matter if you are using a totally different mail program to the sender of the message, you should still be able to transfer just about any type of object.

Although it's early days yet, there is no reason why someone shouldn't be able to attach a piece of video or maybe a slideshow program to an email message in this way. So you get a message about someone's new product and as soon as you have read the mail you get a slideshow or video of the product itself. The ultimate in electronic junk mail or a wonderful and useful communications aid? Hmmm, could be both I reckon. What MIME is becoming very useful for right now is attaching a spreadsheet or word processor file to email, making business communications that much more powerful.

Finding folks

There are a number of tools on the Internet that will help you find someone's Internet address, perhaps the most easily accessible is Finger.

Finger lets you find out information about a system, the people who use that system, and even allows you to find the username of an individual user on a local system.

The information that gets displayed when you finger someone is kept in a "plan" file, and not all systems support these and of course many users may

The result of
a very
interesting
Finger
session.

```
ip> finger idol@well.sf.ca.us
[well.sf.ca.us]
The following includes information on only those WELL users who have
specifically chosen to make information about themselves publicly
available.  For help contact <support@well.sf.ca.us>.

Login: idol                              Name: William Broad
Directory: /home/i/d/idol                Shell: /usr/local/shell/gone
Last login Sun Jul 24 09:14 (PDT) on pts/13 from well.sf.ca.us
Plan:
Mail Address: idol                                Registered: Wed Mar 31 16:24:17 1993
Computers:  PC Clone
Terminal: vt102


Dear Net Surfers:

I'm very sorry if you are in receipt of an automated message from my Well
account, but after almost one year of answering my mail, I've found the task
to be overwhelming. Right now, as I am writing this, my mailbox has over
4000 messages and there is no way I can personally answer all of them without
spending all of my days at the computer.

So, I'm signing off of this account. If you are truly creative, you may be
able to figure out my other account. If not, stay tuned, I am trying to set
up a way to reach all of you in a more general way.

Keep rockin'

lyl libido a.k.a. Billy Idol

April, 1994
```

have an empty plan file. Finger can be useful, but only if the plan information is available. There are disadvantages – fingering a common name may give you screens full of information about users with that name.

Assuming your service provider supports finger, and most do, just type

```
finger [name]@[address]
```

Mail manners

There are a number of unwritten rules regarding the use of email on the Internet, collectively known as email etiquette. Fall foul of them and you face the wrath of the Net Police, so I'm going to write down those unwritten rules (I think that's right, anyway).

○ Use smileys to express the emotion behind the statement. Plain text makes it difficult to ensure that the reader will see something the same way as you meant it, a smiley or two can help. It is amazingly simple to have something interpreted completely wrongly. See the smiley dictionary at the back of this book for reference.

○ Don't use email as a handy method of delivering junk mail quickly around the planet. You may well regret this after the first few thousand angry responses, you will certainly wish you hadn't bothered when your hard disk has become full up with email containing complete unix manuals or the works of Shakespeare! This includes the passing on of chain mail, please don't do it...

○ Don't flame unless you have to (if you are anything like me there will be times when just have to). A flame is a message full of abuse and outrage towards the poster of a particular message you disagree strongly with. Sending a flame usually results in getting one back, and flame wars often occur as a consequence.

○ Don't SHOUT. Composing a message completely in upper case letters is the electronic equivalent of SHOUTING. Don't do it, it makes reading a message very difficult and is universally frowned upon.

○ Don't libel in email, you could find that your message is just as good a piece of evidence as if you had typed it and sent it by snail mail.

Using the Chameleon Mail program

The email program included on the disk with this book is a cut down version of the fully featured mail program that comes with the commercial version of Chameleon (for example there is no support for MIME). However, it is still a very useful email program and will enable you to get those messages moving efficiently.

Before you can start using Chameleon Mail you will need to set up the program properly, and you will require details of gateways and server addresses that your Service Provider will have given you when you opened your account with them.

To set up your email account in Chameleon follow these simple steps:

1)   Select the Mail icon from the Chameleon Sampler program group

2)   A "user login" box will appear, select the Postmaster entry and click
        on the OK button. Don't worry about a password at this stage.

3)   Select the "Mailboxes" entry from the Services menu.

4)   Enter your username, not your full email address.

5)   Click on the Add button.

6)   If you want to keep the Email on your computer secure from prying
        eyes, then enter a password of your choice. This is a password only
        within Chameleon Mail, nowhere else!

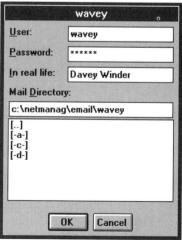

7)   Enter your name in the "real life" box

8)   Enter the path name for your mail directory, each user should have a separate mail directory where all messages will be stored. Then click the OK button, followed by the Save button in the mailboxes window.

9)   Close the mailboxes window.

10)   Close the Mail program.

The next step is to set up Chameleon to work with your mail server, and this is accomplished as follows:

1)   Select the Mail icon from the Chameleon Sampler program group.

2)   Select your username from the "login box".

3)   Enter your password if you have specified one!

4)   Click on the OK button, and then select the Mail Gateway option from the "Network" sub-menu reached from the "Settings" menu (whew!)

5)   Enter the details of your Mail Gateway, this is the host that Chameleon will send outgoing mail to, and you should get this information from your Service Provider.

6)   Click on the OK button, and then select the Mail Server option from the same menu.

7)   Enter the details of your Mail Server, this is the host that stores your incoming mail until you come and collect it. Again, your Service Provider will inform you of the correct address. Enter your username in the "User" box, your password next to "Password", and leave the "Mail Dir" entry blank.

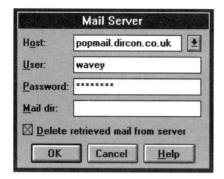

8)   Make sure that you have checked against the box marked "Delete retrieved mail from server" or you will be sent lots and lots of copies of every mail message!

9)   Click on the OK button, and then select the Preferences option from the "Settings" menu.

10)   Click on the "Advanced" button, and set the "From" field to your full email address.

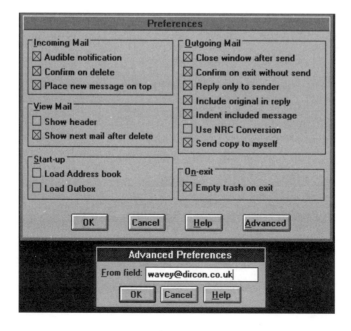

11) Click on the OK button.

Congratulations, Chameleon should now be ready to send Email to the world. But first let's make sure you have done everything correctly and test this by sending Email to yourself.

1) Click on the "Create" button.

2) Enter "A Message From Elvis" in the "subject" field.

3) Click on the "Names" button.

4) Enter your full email address in the "address" field.

5) Click on the "To" button and then "OK".

6) In the lower window, the big one with nothing in it, enter the following text: "I'm gonna sit right down and write myself a letter"

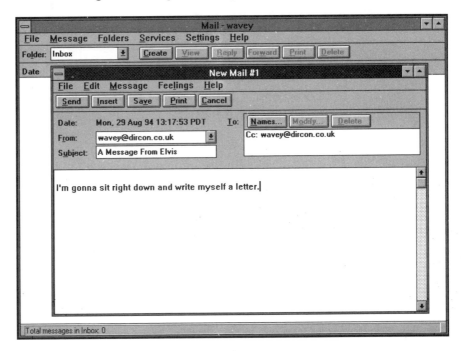

7)   When you have completed the text of your message, select the
        "Send" button.

8)   The mail message you have just composed has now been moved to
        your "outbox" and is waiting to be sent.

9)   Select the "Custom" icon from the Chameleon Sampler program
        group, and click on the "Connect" entry.

10)   Once you a connection to your Service Provider has been established,
        return to the Mail program and select the "Outbox" entry from the
        "Services" menu.

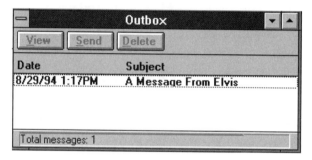

11)   Your message should be sitting in this window, it will have a subject
        entry of "A Message From Elvis".12). Select your message, then click
        on the "Send" button.

13)   Wait about 10 seconds or so after the message entry has vanished
        from your outbox, and then select the "Retrieve Mail" option from
        the "Message" menu.

14)   The message should now appear in your incoming mail folder with a
        small yellow envelope icon to the left of it. Click on the message to
        read it. If a message appears saying "No New Mail" then wait another
        30 seconds and try again, this will most likely just mean that the Mail
        Server is very busy and Email is taking slightly longer to get delivered.

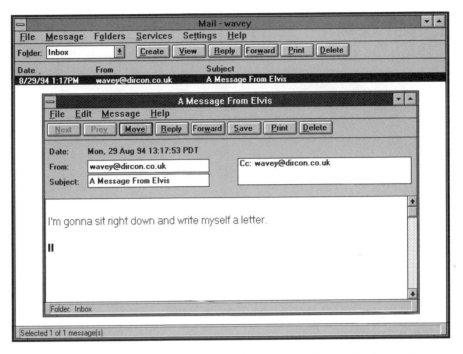

15)   Once you have read your email, the envelope icon will change to an open envelope with letter attached which lets you know the mail has been read.

Chameleon will automatically check for new email every time you start the program. It will also sort email into different predefined folders according to subject matter as specified by certain rules that you can set up. You can use the address book to store all the email addresses you use, although this doesn't support aliases so you can't store **waveydavey@delphi.com** under an entry of Davey Winder for example.

However, for now, you have successfully sent your self email and can explore the other features of the Chameleon Mail program at your leisure.

Email connections

Sometimes the thought of sending email to someone using a different system to yourself, over the Internet, can seem quite daunting. Not surprisingly so as there are many different address formats out there – get it wrong and your important message won't arrive. Even the really big boys in the on-line world, such as CompuServe, can have odd little traits that make email addressing a problem. One of the most common questions about email I get asked is "how can I send email via the Internet to someone on CompuServe?". Read on and you will find the answer to this, and many other possible email addressing problems.

Detailed in this chapter are the correct formats for sending email to and from a number of on-line services, which should hopefully answer most of your mail addressing problems. There are bound to be, however, some services that are not covered here. Indeed, there are many services that are not covered here as I have not bothered with all the systems nobody in the UK has ever heard of, which usually appear in Internet books. This is a short, but hopefully useful list, meant to be used by real people living and working in the real world!

From	AppleLink
To	Internet
Address Format	`user@domain@internet#` (note that address must be less than 35 characters)

From	BBC Networking Club
To	Internet
Address Format	`user@domain`

From	Cix
To	Internet
Address Format	`user@domain`

From	Cix
To	CompuServe
Address Format	`70123.4567@compuserve.com`

From	Cix
To	Delphi
Address Format	`user@delphi.com`

From	Cix
To	Fidonet
Address Format	`username@1.234.567.fidonet.org` (where 1.234.567 is the Fidonet number 1:234/567)

From	CompuServe
To	Internet
Address Format	`INTERNET:user@domain`

From	Delphi
To	Cix
Address Format	`IN%"user@cix.compulink.co.uk"`

From	Delphi
To	Internet
Address Format	`IN%"user@domain"`

From	Fidonet
To	Internet
Address Format	`user@machine.site.domain ON 1:1/31`

From	Internet
To	AppleLink
Address Format	`user@applelink.apple.com`

From	Internet
To	BBC Networking Club
Address Format	`user@bbcnc.org.uk`

From	Internet
To	BIX
Address Format	`user@bix.com`

From	Internet
To	Cix
Address Format	`user@cix.compulink.co.uk`

From	Internet
To	CompuServe
Address Format	`70123.1234@compuserve.com` (note the importance of converting the ',' in the CompuServe account number to a '.' in the mail address)

From	Internet
To	Delphi
Address Format	`user@delphi.com`

From	Internet
To	Fidonet
Address Format	`username@1.234.567.fidonet.org` (where 1.234.567 is the Fidonet number 1:234/567)

From	Internet
To	GreenNet
Address Format	`user@gn.apc.org`

From	Internet
To	IBM
Address Format	`user@vmnode.tertiary_domain.ibm.com`

From	Internet
To	ibmmail
Address Format	`ccsssuuu@ibmmail.com` (where cc=country code, sss=company site,uuu=uniquenumber)

From	Internet
To	Janet
Address Format	`user@domain`

From	Janet
To	Cix
Address Format	`uk.co.compulink.cix::username`

Chapter 7

FTP – File Transfer Protocol

During your travels through the Internet you will probably see the word FTP more than any other. FTP is an acronym for the Internet "File Transfer Protocol", and it is used not only to describe the protocol itself but also the actual physical act of transferring a file, you will quite often hear someone say that you can "FTP that from such and such a site". With the exception of email, FTP is probably one of the most used aspects of the Internet. There are literally millions and millions of files stored on the networks that comprise the Internet – documents, images, sounds, shareware and public domain software, and so on. It stands to reason that you are going to want to download some of these at some stage, and FTP will allow you to do just that.

The Internet doesn't allow you just to log on to any site and download files at will from their computers, that would be plain stupid. You have to specify a username and password when connecting to an FTP site, so as to prevent abuse of the system, which is fine if you have such access privileges to the site you want to connect to. There are, fortunately enough, a large number of sites who actually do want anyone to be able to download files from their systems. Known as Anonymous FTP, these sites generally have a public directory which anyone can access while retaining sensible security restrictions on the rest of their directories. When prompted for a username and password on Anonymous FTP sites, you just enter "anonymous" and your full email address respectively.

When prompted for your email address as a password on Anonymous FTP sites, instead of typing the whole damn thing in you can save time and effort by just typing <username>@ and pressing the carriage return. The remote site already knows where you have made the connection from, so you don't have to type that information.
For example, instead of typing "dwindera@cix.compulink.co.uk" I would just enter "dwindera@".

It doesn't matter what computer you are using to connect to the Internet – be it a PC, Macintosh, or Amiga – FTP will take care of the business of getting the file from where it is stored to your machine. What does matter is the type of Internet connection you have. Well, it matters with regard to how quickly you can get your hands on the file concerned anyway. If you have a direct or dial-in (SLIP/PPP) connection then the file you want to transfer is downloaded straight to your hard disk, this is the fastest and easiest method. However, if you are using a commercial dial-up or terminal connection of the type provided by Cix or Delphi for example, then FTP becomes a slightly more complicated and time consuming process. The files you want to transfer are not FTP'd directly to your computer but rather to your Internet directory on the service providers computer. So FTP becomes a two stage process with you having to download the file, effectively, twice. You may not, of course, realise this as services such as Delphi make the process quite painless by automatically downloading the file to your computer from their computer after it has been FTP'd. The point to remember is that this still involves two downloads, so it is taking twice as long to get that file, and costing you twice as much in on-line charges and telephone bills!

FTP doesn't have to be frightening. A number of client programs make it very easy indeed, like the one included on the Chameleon Sampler with this book for example!

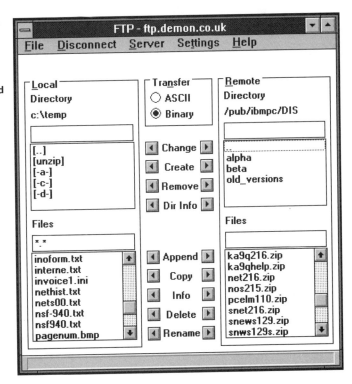

To connect to an FTP site you just need to know the site name, and there are literally ooh, lots and lots (OK, so I hadn't actually compiled the directory when I wrote this bit) contained in the Wavey Davey FTP Directory at the end of this chapter. Select one that looks like it contains files you will be interested in, and assuming you are connected to the Internet use the following syntax from the main prompt:

```
ftp <sitename>
```

For example, if I wanted to get connect to the absolutely massive anonymous ftp site at **wuarchive.wustl.edu** I would type

```
ftp wuarchive.wustl.edu
```

Remember that some sitenames are actually prefixed with the word ftp, for example:
```
ftp.spies.com
```
Don't forget that you still need to enter the ftp command before the sitename, in this case you would type:
```
ftp ftp.spies.com
```

Using FTP

Before we go any further down this particular information avenue, there are several important things you should know about using FTP. You need a basic understanding of the structure of FTP sites and how to move around them, as well as some idea as to just what all those funny filename extensions you will see actually mean. Allow me to explain.

MAKE A
NOTE!

As with most things Internet, FTP sites tend to be running on a UNIX operating system, which means you need to know some basic UNIX commands so you can move around while browsing for files.

In much the same way as you would store different types of files in different directories on your computer, so it is with FTP sites. Files are sorted into different directories and sub-directories according to subject matter, type etc. For the most part you will probably be using Anonymous FTP, and by and large the files available to you will be kept in a directory called "pub" (short for public).

If you ever get stuck when using FTP and can't remember what commands you want, then typing help will usually give you a list of available commands.

Assuming you have successfully connected to an FTP site, the first thing you will need to do is see what the directories are, and you do this by typing

`dir`

This will return a list of directories together with information about them, which you probably won't be too interested in apart from the directory description.

To move to the directory of interest you would type

`cd <directory name>`

Issuing another dir command will then list all the sub-directories available within that directory, and you can move to them using the cd command. If you want to move backwards through a directory structure then you would type

`cdup`

which takes you to the previous directory, and if you ever get confused as to where you are then the command

`pwd`

will tell you the name of the current directory.

So you have now moved through directories and found a file you want to download, so what next? First of all you will need to ensure that the file is transferred using the correct method depending on its type. Most FTP sites default to ASCII transfers, which are fine for text files, however if you want to transfer any other type of file (executable, program, sound, or image) then you will need a Binary mode transfer. You can set this by typing

`binary`

To switch back to an ASCII transfer mode you just type

`ascii`

Let's say for the sake of example that the file you want to transfer is a very nice picture of a dazzling teapot, called daveypot.gif and you have already set the transfer type to binary, your next step is to issue the command that will instigate the file transfer by typing

`get daveypot.gif`

FTP will then start transferring the file to you, and you can monitor the progress of the transfer by watching lots of really interesting # symbols wandering across your screen. Each of these hashmarks represents 1K of data. When the transfer is complete you will automatically be back at the ftp> prompt from where you can carry on transferring or exploring. If you want to transfer more than one file without having to keep issuing get commands, you can use the command

`mget <filenames>`

If you wanted to transfer all files that had a prefix of wavey in the filename, you would type

`mget wavey*`

Once you have had enough of transferring files, you can exit from the FTP session by typing

`quit`

File types

One thing you will notice when you travel around any FTP site is that there are a lot of filename extensions, and some of these may be very confusing to you. Obviously there isn't a problem with such extensions as .txt .doc or .exe but what about .tar or .tar.Z? These file extensions tell you what type of program the file is, .txt is a text file and .exe is an executable program.

MAKE A
NOTE!

On the Internet many files are compressed to form an archive before being stored. This makes the file smaller, therefore cheaper to transfer and more efficient to store. Many of the odd extensions you will see actually refer to the type of archive method used, vitally important if you are going to be able to extract the file you want from the archive.

The following table gives you the low-down on what the most common file extensions mean. You should be able to find the appropriate archiving programs at most Anonymous FTP sites if you don't already have them.

Extension	Archiver
.arc	pkpak
.arj	arj
.gz	gzip
.hqx	binhex 4.0
.lha	lha
.lzh	lha
.pak	Pak
.pit	Packit
.Sit	Stuffit
.tar	tar

.tar.Z	tar and compress
.zip	pkzip
.zoo	zoo
.z	pack
.Z	compress

Viruses

It is a sad fact of life that there are certain unsavoury individuals who have nothing better to do with their time than writing or spreading viruses. It shouldn't come as any surprise, therefore, that these same idiots have realised the power of the Internet for spreading their dirty work. Wavey's golden rule is to CHECK EVERY DOWNLOAD FOR VIRUSES. It can't be said enough, it is much better to be safe than sorry. Most sites do their best to check for any virus infected files, but you can't expect them to be 100% successful in this endeavour. Make sure you have a copy of the latest virus checking software for your particular computer and run it over every file you download. Never execute a file before you have checked it over.

You may already own an Anti Virus Program and not realise it, like the Microsoft one that is supplied with Windows.

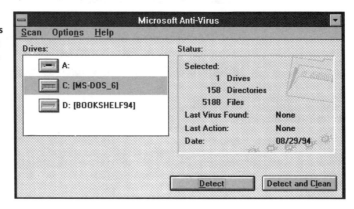

FTP by email

It is also possible to FTP a file using email, so as to save on the actual work of connecting to a site and retrieving a file (if you're a real lazy daisy, that

The easiest method I know of using FTPMail is that open to users of a WinNET UK account.

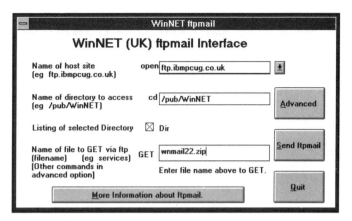

is). While this is pretty damn useful if you don't have an Internet connection, for readers of this book I would suggest sticking to using your Internet account – it's a lot easier, efficient, and a damn sight quicker that way. Unless of course you are using a program such as WinNET which makes FTPMail fairly simple, that is. But for the record, here's how FTPMail (as it is known) works.

Essentially, FTPMail involves sending an email request for a file to a special server, giving the precise details of what the file is and where it is located. The file is then returned to you by email having first been converted to text using a uuencode program and compressed to save on space. If the file is large it will be broken down into a number of such email messages which you will have to piece together and uudecode. In the UK there is a FTPMail server at **ftpmail@doc.ic.ac.uk**

Because you need to know the exact details of what a file is called and the directory structure where it is stored, it is likely that you would first need to make a search using Archie (which can also be done using email) to get these details. This all adds up to a very time consuming process, not only in composing all the email but more importantly in the time it takes for the searches to be made, results returned, and then for the file itself to be emailed to you. Archie is described in some depth elsewhere in this book, so I won't go into detail here.

Using the Chameleon Sampler for FTP

If you are running Windows you can use the Chameleon Sampler program included on the disk that comes with this book. The Sampler comes with a fully working, and very easy to use, FTP program. Now FTP can be as easy as using any file management utility under Windows, like File Manager for example. It's the FTP program that I use almost every single day, so take it from me that it's damn good at its job! Here's how to get those files moving the simple way! Before I start, I am assuming that you have already setup the Chameleon Custom program following the instructions given earlier, and have established that your Internet connection is working satisfactorily. To set up the FTP program, follow these simple steps:

1:   Select the Chameleon Sampler Program Group.

2:   Select the FTP icon, which opens the FTP window.

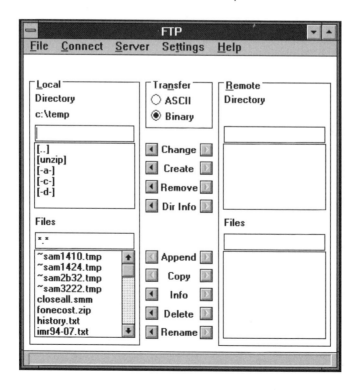

3: Select "preferences" from the "Settings" menu.

4: Select the file management requirements you desire, leaving all boxes checked is your best bet until you are used to the program.

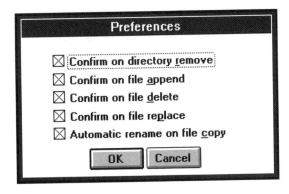

5: Click OK to save the settings.

6: Select "colours" from the "Settings" menu to change the default FTP window colours should you so wish.

7: Select "connection profile" from the "Settings" menu.

8: Click on the "New" button, and you can now add the details of FTP sites you will want to visit on a regular basis. To get started enter the following details which will enable you to connect to the Anonymous FTP server at **wuarchive.wustl.edu**.

Description: WUARCHIVE
Host: wuarchive.wustl.edu
User: anonymous
Password: <your email address>
System: Auto
Account: <leave blank>
Remote Dir: <leave blank>

Local Dir: <the directory on your computer where you want to download files to>.

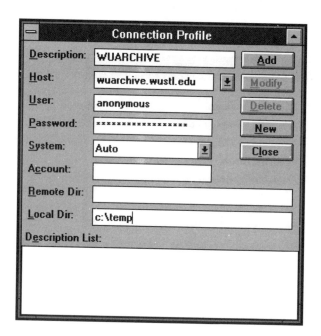

9:      Now click on the "Add" button to save your entry.

The Chameleon FTP Client is now configured and ready for use! To run Chameleon FTP and download files, follow these steps:.

1:      Select the Chameleon Sampler Program Group.

2:      Select the Custom icon, which opens the Chameleon Custom window.

3:      Select the "Connect" menu item, which will connect you to your Internet Service Provider.

4:      Select the Chameleon FTP icon from the Chameleon Sampler Program Group, which opens the FTP window.

5:        Select the "Connect" menu item, which should show
          wuarchive.wustl.edu as the host.

6:        Click on the "OK" button.

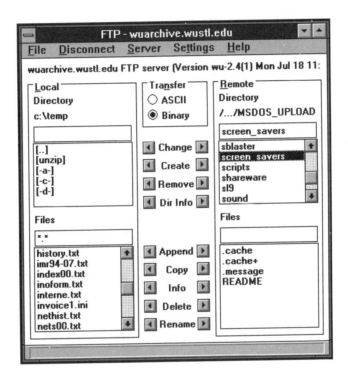

7:        Chameleon will now establish a connection with the FTP server at
          wuarchive, and will display a message letting you know when the
          connection has been made.

8:        You can move through the directories at the FTP site by double
          clicking on their names in the remote directory window, and by
          using theappropriate buttons that point towards that window.

9:        Available files will appear in the files window.

All you need to know about the Internet

10:   Once you have found a file you want to download, first select either the "Binary" or "ASCII" item in the "Transfer" section.

11:   Select the file you want to download by clicking on it.

12:   Select the "copy" button that points at your local directory (the arrow to the left of the word "copy").

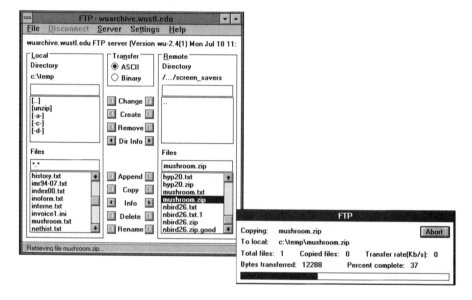

13:   The file transfer will now start, and the progress of the transfer can be monitored by the dialogue box that will appear.

14:   When you have finished transferring files, select the "Disconnect" menu item, and then the "Disconnect" button in the dialogue box that appears.

Congratulations, you have just successfully transferred a file using FTP.

Chapter 8

Wavey Davey's FTP Site Directory

won't even attempt to produce a directory that is comprehensive as new sites appear all the time, and old ones join the great Internet Graveyard. What I have done is try to index a large number of Anonymous FTP sites by subject matter, most of these sites will, of course, hold many files on many different subjects. This directory is just to help get you started, use it as a base camp and have fun exploring!

WHAT
DOES IT
MEAN

I have adopted the use of URLs in the resource directories within this book. A URL is a Uniform Resource Locator, and is becoming the accepted standard method of addressing Internet resources. URLs are incredibly easy to understand – here's my quick explanation. A URL is composed of two parts, the actual resource address and a descriptor to identify the particular Internet resource in question. These two parts are separated by a "://" and everything before this separator is the resource descriptor, everything after it the address. A descriptor may be telnet, http (which refers to World Wide Web), ftp, gopher, or mailto (for mailing lists and Email). For example, if I was pointing you towards a directory called /pub held at the `ftp.demon.co.uk` site, the URL would be:

`ftp://ftp.demon.co.uk/pub`

Remember, it is only the part after the :// separator that you need to actually type, everything before this is just the description of the Internet resource concerned.

Subject: BAGPIPES
Description: Boy are you glad I'm here, because I just know you were hoping I'd tell you where you can find files relating to bagpipes. Weren't you?.
URL: `ftp://cs.dartmouth.edu`

Subject: BEER
Description: Recipes for brewing one's own bevy.
URL: `ftp://ftp.spies.com/Library/Untech/`
            `alcohol.mak`

Subject: BUDDHISM
Description: Lots of information about the Buddhist religion.
URL: `ftp://coombs.anu.edu/coombspapers/`
                 `otherarchives`

Subject: COMPUTER UNDERGROUND DIGEST
Description: CUD is the journal of hacking and cyberspace, and a bloody
                 good read as well.
URL: `ftp://etext.archive.umich.edu/pub/Zines/CUD`

Subject: COMMUNITY
Description: The Computer Communicators' Association. Files relating to
                 CommUnity can be found in this archive, including a
                 membership application form.
URL: `ftp://ftp.demon.co.uk/pub/archives/community`

Subject: COOKING
Description: An archive of recipes.
URL: `ftp://gatekeeper.dec.com/pub/recipes`

Subject: CROWLEY
Description: The texts of Aleister Crowley, one of the Fathers of modern
                 witchcraft.
URL: `ftp://slopoke.mlb.semi.harris.com/pub/`
                 `magick/magick/ Crowley`

Subject: DANCE
Description: Material of interest to dancers and, indeed, those who like
                 dance.
URL: `ftp://ftp.cs.dal.ca/comp.archives/`
                 `rec.arts.dance`

Subject: DEMON
Description: The Demon Internet FTP site where you can find a cornucopia
                 of Internet access tools and documentation.
URL: `ftp://ftp.demon.co.uk`

Subject:	DISABILITY
Description:	You will find something like 40 directories here that cover all types of disability.
URL:	`ftp://handicap.shel.isc-br.com`

Subject:	DISCOGRAPHIES
Description:	Lots of discographies of lots of groups. That is listings of records released rather than graphs of people dancing in a silly manner.
URL:	`ftp://ftp.spies.com/Library/Music/Disc`

Subject:	DISNEY
Description:	Everything Walt Disney is here.
URL:	`ftp://quartz.rutgers.edu/pub/disney`

Subject:	GUITAR
Description:	Guitar chords and tablature in downloadable format.
URL:	`ftp://ftp.nevada.edu/pub/guitar`

Subject:	HUBBLE SPACE TELESCOPE
Description:	Lots of interesting things from Hubble and the Space Telescope Science Foundation.
URL:	`ftp://stsci.edu`

Subject:	INTERNET FAQ
Description:	If you are want answers to even more FAQs than you get in this book (what? surely not possible) then try looking here.
URL:	`ftp://rtfm.mit.edu/pub/usenet/news.answers/internet-service`

Subject:	KAMA SUTRA
Description:	The electronic version of this famous classic guide to love making.
URL:	`ftp://quartz.rutgers.edu/pub/sex/kama.sutra`

Subject: KING ARTHUR
Description: Files, pictures and documentation about King Arthur.
URL: `ftp://sapphire.epcc.ed.ac.uk/pub/camelot`

Subject: KORAN
Description: The Koran in electronic format. This is the Shakir translation of
                 the holy text.
URL: `ftp://quake.think.com/pub/etext/koran`

Subject: MAILING LISTS
Description: A list of all the mailing lists there are. This is the big one, it's
                 bigger than a very big thing that's too big for its boots.
URL: `ftp://ftp.nisc.sri.com/netinfo/`
                 `interest-groups`

Subject: MONTY PYTHON
Description: Scripts and Screenplays from the Monty Python gang.
URL: `ftp://nic.funet.fi/pub/culture/tv+film/`
                 `series/MontyPython`

Subject: ORIGAMI
Description: Instructions on everything from how to make a lovely hat
                 right through to how to spend many a joyous evening folding
                 paper into a life-size replica of Frank Bruno. Well, lots of hints
                 for Origami fans anyway....
URL: `ftp://nstn.ns.ca/listserv/origami-l`

Subject: OTIS
Description: The OTIS project is an ambitious on-line picture gallery, with
                 hundreds of pictures, animations, and files of interest to art
                 lovers.
URL: `ftp://aql.gatech.edu/pub/OTIS`

Subject: PGP
Description: Lots of information about Pretty Good Privacy, the public key
                 encryption utility, can be found here.
URL: `ftp://ftp.uu.net`

Subject: POSTAL CODES
Description: A list of European postal codes. Happy happy joy joy, your life
                   is now complete....
URL: `ftp://nic.funet.fi/pub/doc/mail/stamps`

Subject: PRATCHETT
Description: Loads and loads of files relating to Terry Pratchett and his
                   Discworld novels, nay masterpieces!.
URL: `ftp://ftp.cs.pdx.edu/pub/pratchett`

Subject: TRAINS
Description: Oh yes indeedy, the history of trains, railways, the
                   undergorund system. It's all here and waiting for Arthur
                   Anorak to pop along.
URL: `ftp://quartz.rutgers.edu/pub/railfan`

Subject: UFO'S
Description: Everything relating to UFO's, crop circles, odd and weird
                   things.
URL: `ftp://ftp/spies.com/Library/Fringe/Ufo`

Subject: UNPLASTIC NEWS
Description: An electronic magazine of the distinctly teapot variety.
URL: `ftp://ftp.eff.org/pub/journals`

Subject: VIRTUAL REALITY
Description: Just about everything in the world of virtual reality. Well,
                   virtually.
URL: `ftp://milton.u.washington.edu/pub/`
                   `virtual-worlds`

Subject: WEATHER
Description: Various views of the weather as shown by satellite pictures,
                   updated daily. An excellent resource!.
URL: `ftp://ftp.met.ed.ac.uk/pub/images/jpeg`

Subject: WITCHCRAFT
Description: Lots of texts relating to all aspects of the Wicca religion.
URL: `ftp://nic.funet.fi/pub/doc/occult/wicca`

Subject: WUARCHIVE
Description: One of the biggest Anonymous FTP sites, because of its
                 popularity you might find it difficult to actually get connected
                 to this one.
URL: `ftp://wuarchive.wustl.edu`

Chapter 9

World Wide Web

One of the newest, and certainly most exciting, developments to emerge from the Internet is the World Wide Web. Known most commonly as WWW, but you may also sometimes hear of W3 or just The Web, the World Wide Web is a hypertext based information exploration tool. WWW makes exploring the Internet not only easy but fun too! In fact, once you have set up your browser, WWW is one of the easiest to use Internet tools there is, as well as one of the most powerful.

The home of the Web, on the Web, of course!

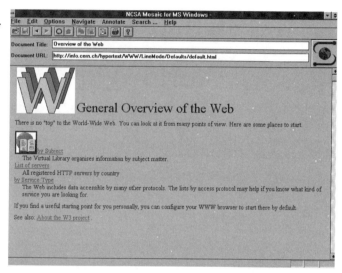

The World Wide Web was developed at the European Laboratory for Particle Physics in Switzerland (better known as CERN for short), and really only started life as recently as 1990. WWW documents are written using something called HyperText Mark-up Language (HTML) which enables hyperlinks to be embedded within them. The hyperlinks allow the user to jump from one piece of information to a related item at a keypress or mouse click, no matter where on the Internet that information is actually stored. This information isn't just text based either, if you are using one of the graphical WWW browsers then you can have sound and vision as well, including the moving image!

The World Wide Web could easily become the de facto interface for Internet use, providing a user friendly window on the Net. As far as I am concerned it is likely to be the "killer application" that attracts more and more people onto the Internet.

There are a number of different ways that you can connect to the World Wide Web:

1)   Using your Internet account to connect to the Web directly with a browser such as Mosaic or Cello.

2)   By Telnetting to a character based WWW browser

3)   Using the WWW browser that has already been set up by your Dial-Up service provider (such as Cix or Delphi)

If you have an account with Cix or Delphi, then using their character based WWW browsers will be the easiest option, as they have already done the hard work of setting everything up. With this access method you generally only need to make a menu choice or enter a simple UNIX command to get things rolling.

Telnetting to a site that offers a character based browser is next on the easy peasy lemon squeezy list. Just find a site (the birthplace of WWW is as good as any, `info.cern.ch`) and follow the on-line instructions.

However, while these are both very easy to use, they lack the capability to display graphics and sound – one of the main features of WWW. This isn't as bad as it may at first seem, as the displaying of graphics slows the browsing operation down quite dramatically. If you are worried about the time spent on-line then maybe the character based approach is best while you are getting used to how things work.

Mosaic for Windows, browsing the World Wide Web. Wow, it's big!

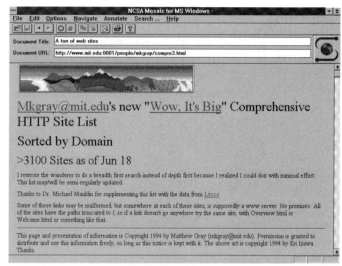

If you want to see the World Wide Web in all its graphical glory, and believe me you really must see it, then you have no option but to get a browser such as Mosaic set up and connect through an Internet service provider who offers a direct connection.

This isn't the simplest method, as the browsers require a certain amount of attention to detail to get the best from them, but don't worry as I'll take you through that process step by step later.

You can find a good selection of World Wide Web browsers for different computer platforms in the archives kept at the following Anonymous FTP site in the UK:

```
ftp.demon.co.uk
```

There are many other places to find these programs, of course, but Demon is as good a place as any to get started

Working your way through the Web

The "line mode" browser

The easiest way to get a feel for the power of the World Wide Web is to telnet to **info.cern.ch**, the place where it all started, and take a look at the character based browser there. OK, so you don't get all the nice pictures and sounds, nor the attractive user interface, but you do get an idea of just how powerful a tool the World Wide Web can be.

Once you are connected you will need to understand a few basic commands to allow you to freely roam through the hypertext linked pages. Here's my quick start guide to help you on your way.

WWW "line mode" browser commands

<number>	Follow the hypertext link defined by the specified number
<return key>	Display next page
back	Return to previous document
bottom	Move to bottom of current document
down	Scroll down a page in current document
find <keyword>	Search for specified text, only available when the browser flags that an index is present
go <pathname>	Go to specified document
help	A list of commands and brief descriptions

The Line Browser at the home of the World Wide Web.

```
                         Telnet - info.cern.ch
 File  Edit  Disconnect  Settings  Network  Help
                                              Welcome to the World-Wide Web
THE WORLD-WIDE WEB

    This is just one of many access points to the web, the universe of
    information available over networks. To follow references, just type the
    number then hit the return (enter) key.

    The features you have by connecting to this telnet server are very
    primitive compared to the features you have when you run a W3 "client"
    program on your own computer. If you possibly can, please pick up a client
    for your platform to reduce the load on this service and  experience the
    web in its full splendor.

    For more information, select by number:

    A list of available W3 client programs[1]
    Everything about the W3 project[2]
    Places to start exploring[3]
    The First International WWW Conference[4]

    This telnet service is provided by the WWW team at the European Particle
    Physics Laboratory known as CERN[5]
        [End]
1-5, Up, Quit, or Help: █
```

info.cern.ch   VT100   25, 24

home	Return to first document read
list	List all links from current document
manual	The on-line manual for the World Wide Web
next	Go to next link in current document
previous	Go to previous link in current document
quit	I bet you can't guess!
recall	List all documents visited so far. Specify a number as an argument to select a specific document from the history list
top	Move to top of current document
up	Scroll up a page in current document
verbose	Toggle "verbose" mode (only really useful if you like lots of code, or are debugging)

The "graphical" browser – Unleashing the power of WWW

It is, as I've already touched upon, the graphical browsers that really make the World Wide Web such an attractive and powerful resource. It's like having an absolutely enormous magazine in front of you, with pictures and sound leaping from the page at the click of a button, a depth of information that we could only dream about just a few short years ago. Make sure you take the little bit of time and effort involved in getting hold of and setting up a graphical browser for your machine, believe me you certainly won't regret it.

The Mosaic Home Page, a great starting place for your explorations of the Web.

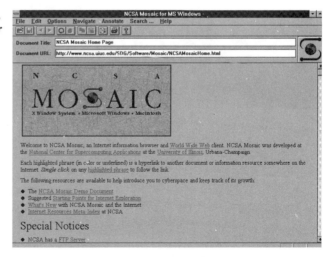

As World Wide Web becomes increasingly popular, so more and more browsers will reach the marketplace. Already many people who were working on the original development of the "Mosaic" browser have moved off to work for companies developing new commercial browsers. Certainly currently the browser of choice for most people is Mosaic. This comes in many flavours, so the likelihood is that whatever machine you are using there will be a Mosaic for you (unless you are somehow accessing the Internet with a Dragon 32 or a Nintendo!).

MAKE A NOTE!

At the moment I know of versions of Mosaic for Windows, Macintosh, Amiga, and X Windows.

The versions available are still Alpha and Beta versions, so you will have to be prepared for them being not quite perfect. In fact, Mosaic does have a tendency to fall over more often than Oliver Reed at a Brewery Open Day. For this reason, some Windows users prefer to use a browser called "Cello" which appears to be slightly more stable. However, as Cello isn't as fully featured as Mosaic, and Mosaic is by far the most popular World Wide Web browser I shall be sticking with it in these examples.

Cello hasn't got quite the same following as Mosaic, but is a nice graphical browser all the same.

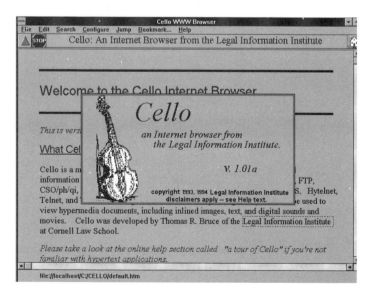

All you need to know about the Internet

Setting up Mosaic

Mosaic is pretty easy to set up, especially if you already have the Chameleon Sampler configured as detailed earlier. You can run Mosaic over the top of Chameleon, using the Chameleon Winsock. If you are not using Chameleon then you will need another Winsock such as the shareware Trumpet Winsock available from just about every FTP site.

WARNING

One thing to watch out for, with regard to the Windows implementation of Mosaic, is which version you are actually running. Some later version require you to be running the win32s software (again available at most FTP sites) as they are 32-bit applications.

If this is a problem for you then make sure the version of Mosaic you get is an earlier 16-bit one. However, I'd recommend going for the later versions as they are much more stable and have many extra features.

The first thing to do once you have downloaded Mosaic and unarchived the file, is to read the documentation. You won't be doing yourself any favours if you skip this part. Next copy the mosaic.ini file to your Windows directory. You will need to edit this file, using any ascii editor such as Notepad. You should be looking to make the following entries:

1)   If you can be contacted by Internet email, then enter your full email
      address in quotes after the E-mail field like this: [Main] E-mail="<your
      full email address goes here>"

2)   If you want Mosaic to automatically load a home page of your choice
      then set the Autoload field to yes, like so: Autoload Home Page=yes
      The Home Page specified by default is the one at the home of NCSA
      Mosaic. However, this site is extraordinarily busy at times which may
      mean you are unable to get connected. You can change the Home
      Page used as default by editing the line:

```
Home Page=http://www.ncsa.uiuc.edu/SDG/Software/Mosaic/¬
NCSAMosaicHome. html
```

Replace everything after "Home Page=" with a page of your choice. Another, even simpler, way of dealing with this possible busy problem is just to set the Autoload field to 'no'.

3)   If you are worried about the time it takes to have images automatically transferred for display, and this can take some time especially if you have a slow connection, then edit the following line to read:
Display Inline Images=no
But take my advice and wait to see if the transfer times are a problem for you first, a graphical browser just isn't the same without the graphics!

4)   If you want a status bar at the bottom of the Mosaic window, and URLs to be displayed in it, then edit the following two lines to read:
Show URLs=yes Status bar=yes

5)   If you want a toolbar at the top of the Mosaic window ensure you have the following line:
Toolbar=yes

6)   Make sure that the section of the mosaic.ini file that is called [Viewers] points correctly to the viewers that you will be using.

That should be enough for you to be able to use Mosaic. Consult the documentation for other changes that you can make to customise the way that Mosaic does its stuff.

Using Mosaic

I'm sure you will now want to see exactly what it is this Wavey Davey bloke has been raving about, and so now's your chance. There are just a couple of steps involved in running Mosaic:

1)   Select the Custom icon from the Chameleon Sampler program group.

All you need to know about the Internet

2)   Assuming you have already set up Chameleon to connect to your Service Provider, select the "Connect" menu option.

3)   Once your connection has been established, double click on the Mosaic icon in whichever program group you have installed it to.

And that is it, you should now have Mosaic running and find yourself at whatever Home Page you have specified. If you don't have a Home Page specified then select a site from the "Wavey Davey's World Wide Web Directory" that appeals to you and enter the URL details as follows:

1)   Select "Open URL" from the File menu.

2)   Enter the details and select OK.

After a short period you should find yourself connected to a World Wide Web page, and the rest is up to you. The real beauty of the Web, of course, is the fact that it is very easy and intuitive to use. Once you have mastered the above basic commands you can just go off and explore, so why not give it a try now?

Having problems?

Although setting up Mosaic is, as you have hopefully found out, pretty easy, there are a few common problems which I can sort out for you right now, at no extra cost.

"Why do I always get the error message "Cannot find winsock.dll" and Mosaic doesn't do anything?"

This is usually caused by the winsock.dll file not being in the windows/system directory, or when its location isn't specified in the PATH= statement of your autoexec.bat file.

"Why do I get the error message that says "Unable to load TCP" all the time?"

This is most likely due to your winsock not being installed properly, resulting in some .dll files being missing or in the wrong place. Check your winsock installation.

"I have installed Mosaic and it is up and running, but whenever I try to connect to a World Wide Web site all I get is the error message of "Failed DNS Lookup".

There are three causes for this error message which refers to the Domain Name Server, the server which resolves Domain names into IP (numerical) addresses.

1)   The IP number of the Domain Name Server is incorrectly entered in Chameleon.

2)   You have mis-typed the URL details, so the name doesn't actually exist.

3)   The Domain Names Server you are trying to connect to has gone down.

Chapter 10

Wavey Davey's World Wide Web Directory

The World Wide Web is, by definition, a massive sprawling beast. Although part of the fun is spending hours tangled in the web, weaving your way around the world, this also costs money. This directory can't hope to be comprehensive, the nature of the Internet sees to that, but I hope it will provide you with some pretty good starting points for your journey. Because the directory is indexed by subject matter, you should also be able to find a site that holds information of interest to you easily and quickly.

MAKE A
NOTE!

The subject title is of my choosing, some sites hold so much information that pigeonholing them is rather difficult, so excuse me if I make an odd decision every now and then (hey, I'm like that!). The important bit is the URL entry, this is the Uniform Resource Locator which points to the site in question. Have a nice trip...

Subject:	3W MAGAZINE
Description:	The WWW pages for Ivan Pope's 3W Magazine which covers all aspects of the Internet.
URL:	`http://www.3W.com/3W/`

Subject:	ANTARCTICA
Description:	The International Centre for Antarctic Information and Research, New Zealand.
URL:	`http://icair.iac.org.nz/`

Subject:	ARCHAEOLOGY
Description:	The Department of Classical Studies, at the University of Michigan.
URL:	`http://rome.classics.lsa.umich.edu/` `welcome.html`

Subject:	AUSTRALIAN ART
Description:	A collection of Australian art from both the Australian National Gallery and the Australian National University.
URL:	`http://www.ncsa.uiuc.edu/SDG/Experimental/` `anu-art-history/home.html` or `http://rubens.anu.edu.au/`

Subject:	BBC
Description:	The BBC Networking Club, TV Listings, talk to BBC producers, feedback on programmes, and a heck of a lot more.
URL:	`http://www.bbcnc.org.uk`

Subject:	BEER
Description:	All you ever needed to know about beer, and lots you didn't.
URL:	`http://guraldi.itn.med.umich.edu/Beer`

Subject:	BOTANY
Description:	The Botany Department of the University of Georgia.
URL:	`http://dogwood.botany.uga.edu/`

Subject:	CAMBRIDGE UNIVERSITY PRESS
Description:	The history of the Campbridge University Press, which dates back to 1534, also extracts from popular titles.
URL:	`http://www.cup.cam.ac.uk`

The Cambridge University Press.

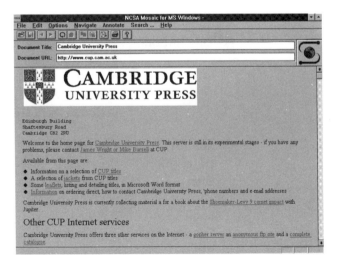

Subject: CHEMISTRY
Description: The Chemistry Department of the University of Sheffield.
URL: `http://mac043025.shef.ac.uk/chemistry/`
                  `chemistry-home.html`

Subject: COKE MACHINES
Description: Yep, those on-line Coke machines that you can "finger"
                  have arrived on the World Wide Web.
URL: `http://www.cs.cmu.edu:8001/afs/cs.cmu.edu/`
                  `user/bsy/www/coke .html`

Subject: COOKERY
Description: An archive of postings to cookery oriented Usenet
                  Newsgroups, containing lots of scrummy recipes.
URL: `http://www.vuw.ac.nz/non-local/`
                  `recipes-archive/recipe-archive.html`

Subject: DANCE MUSIC
Description: Dance music in the UK.
URL: `http://www.tecc.co.uk/tqm/uk-dance`

Subject: DEAD SEA SCROLLS
Description: The World Wide Web Dead Sea Scrolls Exhibition, an
                  excellent on-line version of the Library of Congress
                  exhibition.
URL: `http://sunsite.unc.edu/expo/deadsea.`
                  `scrolls.exhibit/intro.html`

Subject: EDUPAGE
Description: IT news and views, mainly taken from the Internet itself.
URL: `http://www.ee.surrey.ac.uk`

Subject: ELVIS
Description: Elvis is alive and well and living in Cyberspace!.
URL: `http://tamsun.tamu.edu/~ahb2188/`
                  `elvishom.html`

Elvis lives on

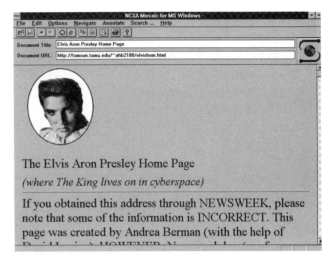

Subject: ETHERNET
Description: Information about Local Area Networks using Ethernet, reading list, faq and more.
URL: `http://wwwhost.ots.utexas.edu/ethernet/ethernet-home.html`

Subject: EXPEDITION
Description: A research expedition about the Belize rain cycle!.
URL: `http://seawifs.gsfc.nasa.gov/JASON/JASON.html`

Subject: EXPO
Description: An amazing collection of WWW "exhibitions".
URL: `http://sunsite.unc.edu/expo/ticket_office.html`

Subject: FANTASY BOOKSTORE
Description: An on-line bookshop with a Science Fiction and Fantasy bias.
URL: `http://www.commerce.digital.com/palo-alto/FutureFantasy/home.html`

Subject: FINANCE
Description: Stock Market quotes, a free "trailer" service for a
                  commercial concern called QuoteCom.
URL: `http://www.quote.com/`

Subject: FINE ART FORUM
Description: An on-line magazine for people interested in the arts.
URL: `http://www.msstate.edu/Fineart_Online/`
                  `home.html`

Subject: GAMES
Description: Links to On-line Games.
URL: `http://wcl-rs.bham.ac.uk/GamesDomain`

Subject: IMPERIAL COLLEGE
Description: The Department of Computing, Imperial College. Leads to
                  lots of useful and interesting places, take a look for yourself.
URL: `http://src.doc.ic.ac.uk`

Subject: INTERNET SOCIETY
Description: Lots of interesting statistics and facts about the Internet can
                  be found at the home of the Internet Society.
URL: `http://info.isoc.org`

Subject: JARGON
Description: A hypertext version of the computing jargon dictionary.
URL: `http://web.cnam.fr/bin.html/`
                  `By_Searchable_Index`

Subject: JEWISHNET
Description: The Global Jewish Information Network.
URL: `http://www.huji.ac.il/www_jewishn/www/`
                  `t01.html`

Subject: JUGGLING
Description: The juggling information service, no less.
URL: `http://www.hal.com/services/juggle`

Subject:	MICROSOFT
Description:	Microsoft's own WWW server.
URL:	`http://www.microsoft.com`

Subject:	MOVIE DATABASE
Description:	Search for information on actors and actresses, films, producers.
URL:	`http://www.cm.cf.ac.uk/Movies/moviewquery.html`

Subject:	MULTIMEDIA
Description:	A veritable treasure trove of multimedia resources.
URL:	`http://cui_www.unige.ch/OSG/MultimediaInfo/`

Subject:	NASA
Description:	The NASA Centre, for all you spacey requirements.
URL:	`http://mosaic.larc.nasa.gov/NASA_homepage.html`

Subject:	NATURAL HISTORY
Description:	A natural history museum exhibit.
URL:	`http://ucmp1.berkeley.edu/welcome.html`

Subject:	NETWORK NEWS
Description:	The InterNIC Internet magazine.
URL:	`http://www.internic.net/newsletter`

Subject:	NEW ZEALAND
Description:	The New Zealand tourist guide.
URL:	`http://www.cs.cmu.edu:8001/Web/People/mjw/NZ/MainPage.html`

Subject:	OTIS
Description:	The OTIS image gallery.
URL:	`http://sunsite.unc.edu/otis/otis.html`

All you need to know about the Internet **.net**

Subject: OXFAM
Description: The official Oxfam "Hunger Web".
URL: `http://www.hunger.brown.edu/oxfam`

The Oxfam Hunger Quiz

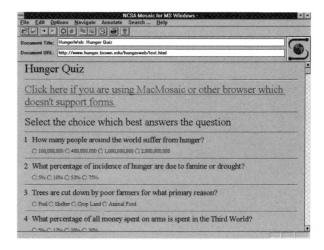

Subject: RADIO
Description: The AM/FM Online UK radio magazine.
URL: `http://www.tecc.co.uk/tqm/amfm`

Subject: RUSSIA
Description: The Friends and Partners project is a joint effort by people
                from both Russia and the USA to help communication
                between the two nations.
URL: `http://solar.rtd.utk.edu/friends/home.html`

Subject: SOVIET ARCHIVE
Description: Exhibition of everything Soviet, very interesting.
URL: `http://sunsite.unc.edu/expo/soviet.exhibit/`
                `soviet.archive.html`

Subject: TRAVEL
Description: Travel information centre.
URL: `http://www.explore.com`

Subject:	WAIS
Description:	The Wide Area Information Server comes to the World Wide Web, and what a lot of Ws that was Wavey!.
URL:	`http://www.wais.com/directory-of-servers.html`

Subject:	WWW FAQ
Description:	A Frequently Asked Questions file.
URL:	`http://www.vuw.ac.nz:80/non-local/gnat/www-faq.html`

Subject:	WWW RESOURCE LIST
Description:	A list of places to visit on the Web.
URL:	`http://www.clark.net/pub/journalism/awesome.html`

Chapter 11

Gopher

A gopher is a burrowing rodent of North and Central America, having a thickset body, short legs, and cheek pouches. It is also a burrowing tortoise. Luckily for me it's an Internet tool as well, otherwise I think I'd be writing the wrong book here.

WHAT
DOES IT
MEAN

Developed by a team at the University of Minnesota (whose mascot is, funnily enough, a gopher) the Internet Gopher is an invaluable tool which provides an easy menu driven way to navigate through the resources of the Internet.

There are lots of alleged reasons for it being called Gopher, from the fact that the University mascot was one, gophers are common in Minnesota, a gopher burrows around, right through to it being a contraction of the phrase "go for this, go for that". Personally I really couldn't care less – it does its job and does it bloody well, does it matter why it's called what it is?

There isn't, in fact, just one Internet Gopher but rather hundreds of Gopher servers and thousands of Gopher clients. The servers are the computers that actually hold and maintain the indexes of resources, and the clients are what you actually use to search those indexes, the friendly menu that you

Using Gopher from Cix. Not as pretty as the Windows Gophers, but just as useful.

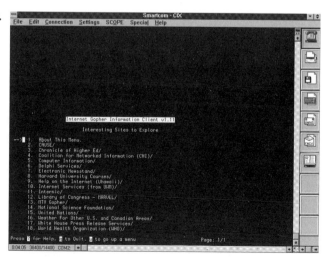

see hides the hard work that the client program is doing, burrowing its way through Gopherspace!

Wavey says watch out for Gopher+ servers, which will soon be available in large numbers and allow you to retrieve formatted text versions of the same document (so one document would be available in PostScript, Microsoft Word, RTF, and ASCII of course). The team at the University of Minnesota are also working on support for on-line forms, which will allow databases, conferencing systems, and more to be attached. There are also security issues such as authentication support which will allow restricted access to selected information. Gopher+ could make Gopher an even more invaluable tool, and real soon now as well.

Gopher presents the user with a very easy to understand menu driven interface to the Internet. It allows you to connect to other computers and search for information, download documents, link you to Usenet Newsgroups, all whilst using the same structured menu approach. Although you may not realise it, every time you select a menu entry you are connecting to another computer, maybe half way across the world, burrowing through what is known as "Gopherspace" to find the information you want.

Using Gopher from the Internet SIG on Delphi, showing some of the gophering options available.

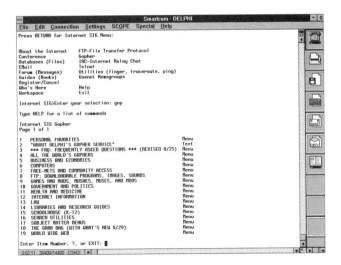

Unlike FTP, where you make a connection to another computer which is kept open while you search through its directories to find the files you want, Gopher opens a connection while it sends your request for information and then closes it, reopening the connection to receive the reply thus saving on network resources in the process. I'd say that Gopher is probably the easiest way for someone who is new to the Net to go exploring. Every type of Service Provider has Gopher clients available so you can get started straight away. Gopher is your very own Internet Librarian, let's see how she works.

Using Gopher

Some Gophers don't actually contain any files themselves, but act as links to other Gophers. So the menu items on the Gopher may actually be gateways to a telnet session, or a search for information using a keyword. However, many Gophers contain information in the form of files, and these files may be text, sound, a binary file and so on. Each menu item, be it a gateway or a file, has an identifier which you will never normally see as the Gopher client hides them nicely out of view. Sometimes you may want to request information about an item, and then you will be faced with an "identifier" with no explanation of what it actually means! Fear not, once again Wavey comes to the rescue, this time with a quick guide to Gopher Menu Types:

Menu Type	Identifier
Archived File (DOS)	5
Binary File	9
BinHexed File (MAC)	4
Directory	1
Error	3
File	0
Image File (GIF)	g
Image File	i
Index Search	7
MIME Email file	M
Phonebook Server	2
Sound File	s

Telnet Session	8
Telnet 3270 Session	T
UUencoded File	6

Not all Gopher clients can actually view all these different file types, for example the standard "text and cursor" type of Gopher can only handle text files. Trying to view a file type not handled by your Gopher client is a waste of time and energy, it may even provide you with a spectacular crash! What I'm trying hard to say here is make sure you know what type of files your Gopher can handle before you start using it. OK?

Most Gophers operate in much the same way, although specific clients may take different approaches to the way they work. Using a character based Gopher such as the Mother of all Gophers at the University of Minnesota will be a different experience altogether from using a graphical client under Windows such as the excellent one that is supplied with the full Internet Chameleon package for example.

The Chameleon Gopher, here pointing me towards a whole wheelbarrow full of UK Gophers.

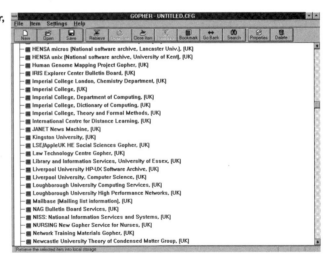

If you want to try the Gopher at its birthplace at the University of Minnesota then you will need to gopher to:

`gopher.tc.umn.edu`

All you need to know about the Internet

If your Service Provider is based in Bedrock and the Managing Director is one Frederick Flintstone Esq., you may find that there isn't a Gopher client implemented in which case you can connect to the Minnesota Gopher by telnet to:

consultant.micro.umn.edu and using "gopher" as your login.

Once connected you will be presented with a fairly self explanatory menu as illustrated below.

The Minnesota Gopher main menu.

As well as just entering the menu numbers in order to navigate around "Gopherspace", there are a whole wheelbarrow full of commands that you can use. Let Wavey reduce that to a medium sized shoebox full, and take a look at the Wavey Davey Gopher Command Guide:

Gopher commands

Navigating Gopherspace

Use the following arrow keys to move around, and then just press return when you want to look at a document.

Up	Move to previous line
Down	Move to next line
Right	Select current item
Left	Exit current item
> or +	View next page
< or -	View previous page
m	Return to main menu

MAKE A
NOTE!

**You don't need to press "enter" whilst at the Gopher menus, just typing
in the commands as shown is enough**

Bookmark Commands

Bookmarks are used to pinpoint interesting places on your travels, and allow
you to get straight to a specific Gopher menu rather than go through all the
menu options you had to first time around. In effect what you end up with
is your own personalised Gopher Menu, and it really is a damn handy
feature. Unfortunately not all Gopher clients support this feature, so make
sure yours does!

a	Add the current item to the bookmark list
A	Add the current directory or search to the bookmark list
v	View the bookmark list
d	Delete a bookmark from the list

Other Useful Gopher Commands

D	Download a file
n	Find next search item
O	Change your options
q	Quit (with confirmation)
Q	Quit (no confirmation)
s	Save current item to a file
=	Display information about current item
/	Search for a menu item

**Wherever possible use a Gopher Client rather than connecting by
telnet. A client is usually much faster, a telnet connection to a Gopher
may end up in extremely slow response times due to the heavy loads
that Gophers experience.**

Going Gophering graphically

Or put another way, making life easy for yourself. The "text and cursor"
type Gopher clients do their job, and do it very well, but they are not the
prettiest creatures to emerge from the Internet neither are they capable of
exploiting the full capabilities of Gophers. If you want to see Gopherspace in
all its visual and aural glory, then you need a graphical Gopher client. I really
rather like the one that comes with the full blown Internet Chameleon
package (see the back of the book for a special purchase offer), and readily
admit that since installing it I rarely use the old character based clients.

The main advantages of a graphical Gopher are:

1) Ease of use. Just point and click, as simple as using a Windows directory
utility. There is no need to learn a command set, just point and go (take
two Gophers into the shower? Not me...).

**Chameleon Gopher
makes Gophering dead
simple. Here I've found a
map of the current
weather in the UK, just
by a process of a few
mouse clicks through a
directory style menu
listing.**

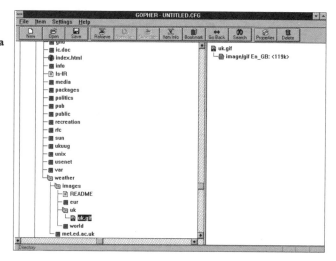

2) Power. Provided you have set up the file associations, just like using File Manager in Windows 3, then different file types are recognised and dealt with automagically. This means that text files will be read through a text viewer, whilst GIF images will be seen with the associated image viewer. What it all boils down to is that Gopher comes alive with images and sound as well as text!

Chapter 12

Wavey Davey's Going Gophering Directory

Subject:	ACRONYMS ON-LINE
Description:	An on-line acronym dictionary for all those obscure computer terms.
URL:	`gopher://info.mcc.ac.uk`

Subject:	AIDS
Description:	Information about Aquired Immune Deficiency Syndrome.
URL:	`gopher://selway.umt.edu 700`

Subject:	ALLERGIES
Description:	The National Institute for Allergy and Infectious Disease.
URL:	`gopher://gopher.niaid.nih.gov/1`

Subject:	ASCII ART
Description:	Acollection of the best and worst in ASCII art, that is pictures that are drawn completly using text characters.
URL:	`gopher://pfsparc02.phil15.uni-sb.de`

Subject:	BIBLE
Description:	This is the King James version, which probably means more to you than it does to me!
URL:	`gopher://joeboy.micro.umn.edu`

Subject:	BOOKSHOP
Description:	The On-Line Bookstore, selling electronic texts, what else?
URL:	`gopher://akasha.tic.com`

Subject:	BRITISH LIBRARY
Description:	The British Library is now on-line with this gopher server that conatins information about the libarary and events held there.
URL:	`gopher://portico.bl.uk`

Subject:	CAMBRIDGE UNIVERSITY PRESS
Description:	Information for authors, details of publications, etc.
URL:	`gopher://gopher.cup.cam.ac.uk`

Subject:	CIA WORLD FACTBOOK
Description:	The US Central Intelligence Agency annual report, which contains a wealth of knowledge about almost 250 nations.
URL:	`gopher://gopher.micro.umn.edu`

Subject:	CYBERPUNK
Description:	A host of Cyberpunk related articles.
URL:	`gopher://wiretap.spies.com`

Subject:	DATABASES
Description:	Where to find commercial and free databases on the Internet.
URL:	`gopher://sunic.sunet.se`

Subject:	DEAFNESS
Description:	Resources for deaf people, but with a USA bias unfortunately.
URL:	`gopher://cl.msu.edu`

Subject:	DISABILITY INFORMATION
Description:	Information about disability related issues.
URL:	`gopher://val-dor.cc.buffalo.edu`

Subject:	EFF
Description:	The Electronic Frontier Foundation has its own gopher.
URL:	`gopher://gopher.eff.org`

Subject:	EYE WEEKLY
Description:	A Toronto arts newspaper, back issues of which are available from this gopher.
URL:	`gopher://gopher.io.org`

Subject:	HISTORY TODAY
Description:	What happened on this day in history?
URL:	`gopher://uts.mcc.ac.uk`

Subject:	IMPERIAL COLLEGE
Description:	The Imperial College, Department of Computing, gopher. Lots of interesting things here, just connect and have a look around.
URL:	`gopher://src.doc.ic.ac.uk`

Subject:	JOKES
Description:	A massive jokes database that can be searched against any keyword you care to enter.
URL:	`gopher://uts.mcc.ac.uk/Gopher Services/ The Joke File`

Subject:	KIDLINK
Description:	This is a project for children between the ages of 10 and 15 years to encourage them to get involved in comms technology. Adults are not allowed, even big kids like Wavey Davey.
URL:	`gopher://kids.ccit.duq.edu/KIDLINK Gopher`

Subject:	MAASTRICHT TREATY
Description:	The text of the Maastricht Treaty.
URL:	`gopher://wiretap.spies.com`

Subject:	MOVIE DATABASE
Description:	An on-line film database which you can search for information about movies, producers, actors, scripts. It works really well, I've used it a lot recently.
URL:	`gopher://info.mcc.ac.uk/Miscellaneous items/Film Database`

Subject:	MUSICALS
Description:	The lyrics to a number of famous musicals including Les Miserables, Phantom of the Opera, Rocky Horror Picture Show, and Eric Makes a Teapot. I might have made one of those up though…
URL:	`gopher://quartz.rutgers.edu`
Subject:	NURSING
Description:	Yes, a gopher for nurses and nursing issues.
URL:	`gopher://crocus.esv.warwick.ac.uk`
Subject:	OXFORD UNIVERSITY LIBRARY
Description:	Texts from the Oxford University library, a massive resource.
URL:	`gopher://gopher.lib.ox.ac.uk/00/Info/OLIS`
Subject:	PHOTOGRAPHY
Description:	The Panix Photographic Database containing mainly technical information and advice about photography.
URL:	`gopher://gopher.panix.com`
Subject:	PROJECT GUTENBERG
Description:	Classics of literature in electronic format.
URL:	`gopher://gopher.umn.edu`
Subject:	REN AND STIMPY
Description:	Oh Happy Happy, Joy Joy, Happy Happy, Joy Joy. A haven for all fans of Ren and Stimpy.
URL:	`gopher://quartz.rutgers.edu/` `Television and Movies`
Subject:	SPORT
Description:	A gopher with a large sports section, which has a refreshing UK bias including such things as football and cricket.
URL:	`gopher://govan.cent.gla.ac.uk`

All you need to know about the Internet

Subject: STERLING
Description: A collection of texts by Bruce Sterling, Daddy of
                   Cyberpunk.
URL: `gopher://gopher.well.sf.ca.us`

Subject: TELEVISION
Description: Programme and product information.
URL: `gopher://uts.mcc.ac.uk/Gopher Services`

Subject: THESAURUS
Description: Project Gutenburg bring you the Roget's Thesaurus in its
                   entirity.
URL: `gopher://uts.mcc.ac.uk/`
                   `Experimental and New Services`

Subject: UNITED NATIONS
Description: The United Nations gopher, with everything you could
                   want to know about the, er, United Nations.
URL: `gopher://gopher.undp.org`

Subject: VIRUSES
Description: Lots of information about computer viruses, Internet
                   viruses, and how to protect yourself against them.
URL: `gopher://wiretap.spies.com/Wiretap Online`
                   `Library/Technical Information`

Chapter 13

What's it all about, Archie?

As another chapter heading goes flying mercilessly over the heads of our readers, and Wavey Davey just shows how old he really is, let's take a look at one of the most used Internet tools around.

WHAT
DOES IT
MEAN

Archie is a very useful Internet tool developed by the McGill School of Computer Science in Canada. Its name is derived from the word "archive" which is most appropriate as Archie will search for the whereabouts of any file stored in any public archive site on the Internet, in other words all the Anonymous FTP sites.

Did I say Archie was very useful? I meant to say it is one of the most bloody useful things ever to come out of Canada!

If you think how difficult it can be finding a file on your hard disk sometimes, and say you hard disk is 540Mb in size, then try and think how difficult it can be finding a file on a network of computers with a storage capacity of a Gigabyte or two. Now sit down and think how impossible it would be trying to locate a file on the Internet, all those networks linked together offering thousands of Gigabytes of storage, million upon million of files. It is as difficult as finding a small pointy thing in a large amount of dried grass, believe me.

Archie in action, searching for Elvis.

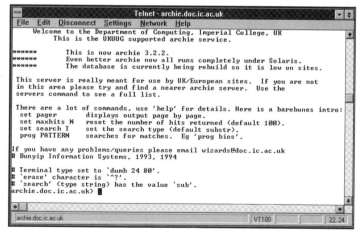

Archie lets the end user query a database containing details of files at more than 1,000 Anonymous FTP sites, and returns a list giving the precise details of where any files that match can be found, right down to directory paths. Using Archie is dead simple, but there are different ways to go about it.

MAKE A
NOTE!

Archie will tell you if a file exists for FTP from the Internet, and what's more will tell you where to find it as well!

1) You may have an Archie client already installed by your Service Provider. Ask them if this is the case, or just type "archie" and see what happens!

2) You can telnet to an Archie server, there are lots of them around but why not try a very popular site in the UK, **archie.doc.ic.ac.uk** using archie as a login name.

3) You can search the Archie database from within a Gopher, so as to make the job even simpler!

**Using Archie
from a Gopher.**

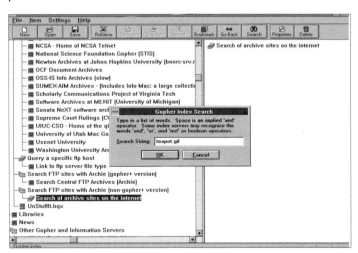

4) Finally you can use Archie by email, sending a message to **archie@doc.ic.ac.uk** leaving the subject line blank but including "prog <filename>" in the message text.

Search me

Before you actually start using Archie, it may be an idea to give some thought to the sort of search that you would like to perform. There are four search types that you may use, and they are:

exact	Requires the exact filename of the file you are looking for
regex	Archie will treat some of the characters typed in the search string as wildcards, according to UNIX regular expressions. If you don't know what this means, then don't use it!
sub	A non case sensitive search for filenames containing or matching the specified string.
subcase	A case sensitive version of sub

Use the sub search category whenever possible, it's the easiest method of finding the file you want.

Once connected to Archie there are a variety of command options open to you. Some of the more useful or common ones include:

bugs	Displays a list of all currently known bugs in the Archie system
help	Lists all valid commands, don't be afraid to use it
list	Reports all Internet sites stored in the Archie database, including the last date that the information on each site was updated
mail	Use this command to send the output of the last command to a specified email address. Useful for emailing the results of file searches to yourself
prog	Probably the most important of the commands, prog is the little beauty that initiates the Archie database search for the specified filename

Archie doesn't accept DOS wildcards, so although you could find the file "teapot.gif" by searching for both teapot.gif and teapot. Using tea*.gif wouldn't work.

set	Use this command to set parameters for use during the Archie session
set mailto	Set a default mail address, allowing the mail command to be used without further arguments
set maxhits	Restricts the number of matches made in any Archie search, the default is 1000 "hits"
set pager	Turn on screen paging
set search	Defines what type of search Archie should perform – choose from exact, regex, sub, and subcase
set sortby	Sets the order in which the output of an Archie search is listed – choose from none, filename, hostname, size, and time
set term	Define the terminal type that you are using
servers	This returns a list of all current Archie servers
show	Display the value of a given variable
site	Lists all the files which are available for FTP from a specified host
unset	Use this if you should ever want to turn off a Boolean variable, which is pretty likely
unset pager	Turn off screen paging
whatis	This command searches a software description database containing names and short descriptions of software resources on the Internet

Chapter 14

Telnet

Telnet is a tool that enables you to connect to another computer that is on the Internet. "Whoa there Wavey, does this mean that anyone can connect to any computer on the Internet?" I hear you cry. In a word, NO. You can sleep well at night, assured by the fact that you can only use Telnet to connect to public accessible computers, or computers where you actually have an account. Once connected to these computers you can act as if you were actually directly connected to them, it's like sitting in front of a computer on your desk and using it with the very slight difference that the computer itself can actually be on the other side of the planet! A related program, called tn3270, allows you to "Telnet" to IBM Mainframe computers that expect a 3270-type terminal.

A typical Telnet session, here I'm connecting to TWICS, an on-line system in Tokyo, by way of a local telephone call.

 You can use many Gophers to easily Telnet to lots of systems just by selecting a menu item. See the Gopher chapter for details of how to use this tool, and sites to connect to.

Telnet is very useful in a real world sort of way. For example I have accounts on computer systems around the world and these would make me entitled to use the British Telecom VIP suite if I dialled them direct every time I logged on. However, using Telnet I can connect to my Internet Service Provider using a local call, and then Telnet to the on-line system in San Francisco or Japan from my local call rate connection!

There are also a large number of public databases such as ERIC and CARL which you can use, free of charge, by Telnetting in. ERIC is the Educational Resources Information Centre and is a United States Department of Education sponsored service. It provides a database of articles relating to education in the US, but also such delights as a database containing the full works of Shakespeare. CARL is the Colorado Alliance of Research Libraries and it has a database called UnCover2 which provides a document delivery service with access to more than 10500 different journals.

Using Telnet

Using Telnet is really quite simple, all you need to do is specify the address of the system you want to connect to. So if I want to connect to the Compulink Information Exchange (Cix) and use my account there, I would just type

```
telnet cix.compulink.co.uk
```

Sometimes responses can be extremely slow when using Telnet to connect to a busy system. This results in it taking several seconds, sometimes even minutes, for your keyboard input to be displayed on screen, and the same for output from the remote system. Unfortunately this is due to heavy network traffic and there is nothing you can do but try again later.

Quite often you will find that a host system allows public Telnet access to only a certain part of their service, and requires you to specify a "port number". All this does is enable you to connect to a certain part of the system, without gaining access to anywhere else. The port number needs to be entered after the address when you use Telnet, for example the Cix Discworld MUD runs on port 4242 so you would need to type

```
telnet mud.compulink.co.uk 4242
```

Once you have issued your Telnet command you will, if you have
successfully connected to the remote computer, be asked for your login
username and password. Most public sites will ask for a publicly known
password and login name, the nicer systems will tell you what these are and
prompt you for them. Some may even let you straight in without this
pretence of security, although this is less common these days.

**When you have finished your Telnet session you have to log off the
remote computer, but this may not always end your Telnet session. To
exit cleanly from Telnet if you find yourself stuck in cyberspace, type
Ctrl-]. This will place you back at the Telnet prompt from where you can
type Quit to get back to your Internet prompt.**

Using the Chameleon Sampler to Telnet

The Chameleon Sampler included with this book features both Telnet and
TN3270 tools, ideal if you are a Windows user. To open a Telnet session
using Chameleon just follow this easy example:

1)   Select the Custom icon from the Chameleon Sampler program
      group.

2)   Select the Connect menu item.

3)   Once your Internet connection has been established, click on the
      Telnet icon from the Chameleon Sampler group.

4)   Select the Connect menu item.

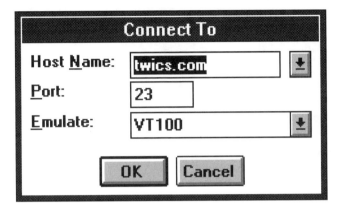

5)   Select the system you want to connect to from the Host Name box. You could use the name as shown in the example screenshots – this is a real hands on example you know!

6)   Press Enter, and Chameleon will try to establish a connection to the specified host system.

7)   Follow the on-screen prompts to navigate your way through the system you are connected to.

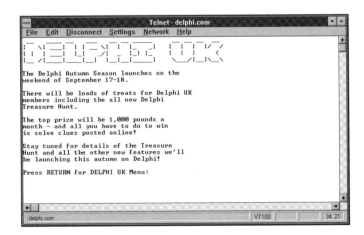

8)   When you have finished, select the Disconnect menu item.

If you can't see what you are typing while in a Telnet session, you need to enable local echoing. Type Ctrl-] to get to the Telnet command prompt, and then enter

`set echo`

and press return. Press return a second time and you will be back at your Telnet session and able to see what you are doing.

Chapter 15

Wavey Davey's Tiny Telnet

Directory

In an attempt to get you started on your journey down Telnet Avenue, and no more, here is a very short list of some useful and interesting places you can connect to using Telnet.

Subject: ANCIENT HISTORY
Description: The Princeton University Library archives. To connect press "Return Key" and when you see the "#" sign, type call 500.
URL: `telnet://pucable.princeton.edu`

Subject: ARCHAEOLOGY
Description: The National Archeological Database contains more than 100,000 reports of archaeological investigations, which can be searched using various criteria. Use the login of nadb.
URL: `telnet://cast.uark.edu`

Subject: BRITISH CONSTITUTIONAL LAW
Description: The University of Texas law library archives, use the login of Library.
URL: `telnet://tallons.law.utexas.edu`

Subject: COOKIES
Description: Not the type that you eat, but those wonderful quotes, sayings, thoughts, pieces of nonsense that change every day. This is the Internet version, every time you Telnet to the Cookie Server it will show you a different, random, Cookie.
URL: `telnet://argo.temple.edu 12345`

Subject: DICTIONARY (ENGLISH)
Description: You will find a decent English dictionary on-line at the University of Michegan library. When asked which host you want, reply Help.
URL: `telnet://cts.merit.edu`

Subject: ELECTRONIC NEWS
Description: The Electronic News Stand provides access to many different electronic journals etc. Login as news.
URL: `telnet://enews.com`

Subject: ERIC

Description: The Educational Resources Information Centre database of interest to teachers, or indeed anyone interested in educational matters Use the login of sonia.

URL: `telnet://sklib.usask.ca`

Subject: FRIENDS AND PARTNERS

Description: A project aimed at aiding communication between the Russian and American people. Use the login of friends.

URL: `telnet://solar.rtd.utk.edu`

Subject: GAMES SERVER

Description: This is a must for any fans of on-line gaming. Games available include such classics as Tetris and Nethack. Use the login of games.

URL: `telnet://castor.tat.physik.uni-tuebingen.de`

Subject: INTERNIC

Description: InterNIC provides a number of services aimed at helping you to get connected and actually use the Internet. Also directories of Internet sites and resources. Use the login of guest.

URL: `telnet://ds.internic.net`

Subject: NASA

Description: How many ears has Mr Spock got? The answer is three, a left ear, a right ear, and a final frontier. Answers to many much more useful astronomical questions can be found at the NASA Extragalactic Database. Use the login of ned.

URL: `telnet://denver.ipac.caltech.edu`

Subject: PMC-MOO

Description: This is the Postmodern Culture MOO, a virtual reality environment where you can talk and interact with various odd people in real time.

URL: `telnet://dewey.lib.ncsu.edu`

All you need to know about the Internet

Subject: QUOTATIONS

Description: The Oxford Dictionary of Familiar Quotations in a searchable on-line format. Once connected you want to go to "libarary" and then "reference".

URL: `telnet://info.rutgers.edu`

Chapter 16

Other applications and tools

There are a number of tools and applications other than those which could be grouped together as the "big boys" of the Internet. And just because they are small and simple, doesn't mean they should be overlooked as they may well be right up your information superhighway!

Ping

I've used this little program so many times in the past few years that I couldn't possibly keep count, but it was only when writing this book that I actually found out what Ping stands for. Of course, when I discovered it was Packet InterNet Groper I rather wished I hadn't bothered!

Ping is very useful for checking that the computer you're connected to is actually talking to the Internet, or any particular system on the Internet for that matter. Ping is a network diagnostic tool that works by sending a "echo request" to a named site and displaying the results of the "echo reply", the exchange of echoes is known as pinging. Sometimes you cannot connect to An FTP site, or Telnet to a remote system and get quite frustrated wondering what you are doing wrong. Ping can ease your mind by checking that the site is actually working OK for you, and thus save you lots of time spent wasted trying to fix something that isn't broke!

Pinging Cix, fun isn't it?

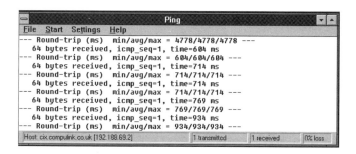

To use the Ping program supplied with the Chameleon Sampler disk, select the Ping icon from the Chameleon Sampler program group. Select "Start" and enter the name of any known site in the "Host" box. For example, enter "**delphi.com**" or "**cix.compulink.co.uk**". If the site is working

OK, and the computer that converts numerical IP addresses to the easier domain name format (called a nameserver) is working as well, you should get a message back which reports "1 transmitted, 1 received, 0% loss". If you get a message of "Failed to resolve host" then something is generally wrong, most likely you have the wrong information entered in the domain server section of the Chameleon Custom program although you may have entered the hostname wrong or the host site may just be down.

Finger

Probably the easiest command you can use while at the helm of your Internet connection is "finger". You can finger anyone on the Internet, although the response isn't guaranteed or even predictable sometimes.

MAKE A
NOTE!

Some on-line systems disable "Finger" access for reasons of user privacy, one such example being Delphi.

Many users over the Internet don't have a plan file, without which no information can be displayed. So don't be too surprised if you find you can't finger a friend in Cyberspace.

The finger application displays information about a specified user on a particular host, including such details as login name, real name, and times of last login etc. Users can set up a document called a plan file which is kept in their home directory and the contents of which will be displayed when anyone fingers them. Some users do this to great effect, advertising their services, or just making a totally teapot statement on life. In recent years, however, the finger command has gathered a lot of publicity as many sites set up plan files for a specific username which delivers information much like a database query would.

For example, fingering **nasanews@space.mit.edu** will return a list of recent NASA press releases, while other sites will give you earthquake reports, the day today history snippets, even FAQ files and the like. Probably the weirdest use of finger has to be the numerous "Internet Coke Machines" that have sprung up. The story goes that students were fed up walking from their halls of residence down to the Coke Machine only to find that the machine had no change, or the drinks were too warm, or it had run out of their favourite flavour drink. Never to be out-anoraked, these guys went and literally connected the Coke machines to the Internet so they could check out all the information using the computer and modem in their rooms, before going down to the machine itself. Word soon spread and now you

Fingering a real live Coke machine on the Internet (live? what am I talking about, huh?)

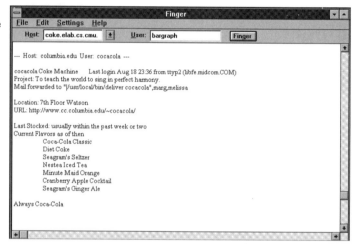

A slightly more useful case of fingering.

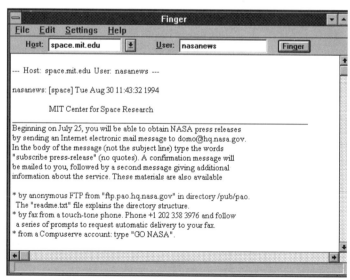

can Finger lots of Coke machines at Universities all over the United States. Not very useful, but certainly an interesting diversion!

Netfind

Netfind tries to address a problem with the Internet. Because it is just so massive how on earth do you find someone on it? Written by Mike Schwartz of the University of Colorado, Netfind requires you to enter the first, last, or use name of the person you are trying to locate followed by any number of "keys". Each key helps to narrow the search by stating where the person works, such as which University or Government department, which country and so on. A typical Netfind search for someone by the name of Norbert Noddy, who works for Imperial College in the Sciences department, would take the form of

netfind noddy Imperial College Science

There are currently a number of Netfind gateways on Gopher servers, with more on the way, so you may be able to use the service from your favourite Gopher. If not, then you can always telnet to a Netfind client such as the

A typical Netfind search, this one was accessed from Delphi.

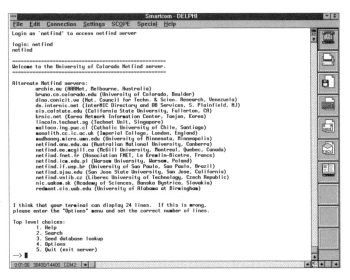

one at Imperial College here in the UK, using netfind as the login name. The address of the Imperial College Netfind client is

monolith.cc.ic.ac.uk

The main problem with Netfind, however, is due to the lack of databases for it to search for this user information. Much of the information is very USA biased (hey what a surprise, folks) and so using Netfind can be a very hit and miss affair. If we're lucky, Netfind databases will continue to be updated and start to become more effective. It would be a shame for such a potentially useful utility to go the way of others before it. Knowbot was one such tool, serving much the same purpose, that is now all but useless as the information contained on its databases is so out of date!

Whois

Perhaps the largest database of Internet organisations and users is located at the InterNic Registration Services host at **rs.internic.net** You can search this database using Whois to return detailed information, unfortunately this will be mainly restricted to network administrators and organisations as that is what the InterNic database holds details of. However, as more and more details are added to the database then WHOIS could certainly become an even more useful tool than it is now.

Whois that
masked man?

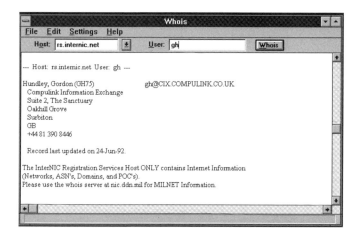

Veronica

You will have read the chapter about Gophers by now, and if you haven't then go back and read it at once!

OK, so now you know what a Gopher is, and how useful a tool it can be. The trouble is that as more and more Gophers have appeared on the Internet, so the task of searching through the Gophers gets ever more time consuming. In fact you may say that you need a Gopher to get through all the Gophers, let alone the Internet beyond.

Enter Veronica, for she fulfils this role. Veronica works in much the same way as a Gopher, but keeps an index of Gopher items thus allowing keyword searches of the titles it holds.

If you were to enter the word "teapot" then Veronica would return a menu of 100s of Gopher menu items that contain that keyword. To connect to the Gopher that looks of interest you just select the relevant item from the Veronica menu. Most Gophers have Veronica listed as a menu item, so check it out and you won't regret it.

Can Veronica find Elvis? Stay tuned to this channel to find out...

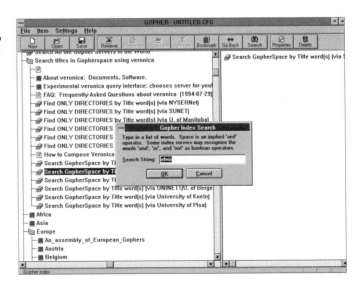

**...The answer is
yes, it would seem.**

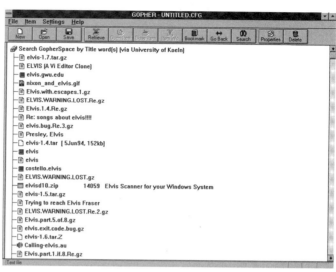

Wide Area Information Servers

A bit of a mouthful that, so not surprisingly Wide Area Information Servers
are only ever referred to by the acronym of WAIS. This tool differs from the
likes of Archie or Gopher in as much as it allows you to search for text
contained within documents such as FAQ files, Usenet Newsgroups, text
files, rather than just the name of a file or directory. WAIS will let you search
for specific information from many different databases, held at different
locations. Because there are, obviously, thousands of different databases
holding textual information across the Internet, there are also an incredible
number of different searching methods for performing searches of them.
WAIS tidies this up for you and lets you search these differing databases
using the one single, simple, interface.

Because WAIS is searching for a keyword among millions of words, it can
take some time to perform a search and return the results to you. Obviously
the more specific you are in your set of keywords to search, the better the
chances of getting a good match to your needs. Unfortunately WAIS cannot
perform Boolean searches, that is where you can use AND, IF, and OR
statements within your search criteria.

WAIS searches can take some time, but the results are usually worth the wait.

For example, if you ask WAIS to search for ITSY AND BITSY it will all documents that contain the words Itsy, Bitsy, and AND rather than documents only containing both ITSY and BITSY. However, all is not doom and gloom because WAIS is pretty clever in other aspects. Like the fact that it will give each document in the list it returns a score out of 1000 depending on how closely it reckons it matches your requirements. Better still is a feature called "relevance feedback" which lets you mark the documents in the list that you feel are most relevant to your needs, and then WAIS will go away and look for other documents that are similar to those ones. By using the relevance feedback system you can get very specific and useful documents, eventually!

Chapter 17

Usenet

If you have ever used a Bulletin Board System, or maybe you have been a member of Cix, CompuServe or Delphi, then you will be familiar with the idea of conferences, forums, and message areas. Places where you can post a message about a defined subject and expect and expect other members within that area to join in the conversation over a period of time.

These message areas, of whatever kind and at whatever site, have always been popular places for people to meet on-line, get to know each other, meet new people, and maybe actually learn something as well. Of course, the usefulness of such conferences and forums (or should that be fora or maybe fori?) is dependant to a large degree on the number of people who actively participate. Think of Usenet as an absolutely enormous message based bulletin board, with over 50Mb of text or in excess of 30,000 messages being posted every single day of the year (and before you get your calculator out I can tell you I've worked out the yearly figures and they add up to more than a hill of beans). Get the picture? Well let's focus in a bit...

Reading Usenet Newsgroups with Demon, one of the most popular methods for UK Usenet fans.

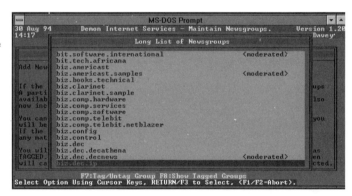

Usenet was developed by two American university students, Tom Truscott and Jim Ellis, who wanted to let people on different computers exchange messages in a way that would be conversational, a sort of on-line discussion group. The software they came up with was the basis of what Usenet has become, after going through many many versions and being used by millions of people worldwide.

Usenet comprises thousands of newsgroups, each covering a specific subject, and within each newsgroup are posted the articles that you read and respond to.

To get to each newsgroup you have to "subscribe" to it, and this won't cost you anything but your time despite the terminology, and the newsgroups available will depend on your Internet service provider. Many service providers offer a full Usenet service, or "feed" as it is known, so you can choose to subscribe to any newsgroup you may hear of. However, others have a restricted or censored feed and so your choice of available newsgroups is then more limited.

It is worth noting that Usenet has become a term used to describe the general principle of newsgroup distribution, and in fact many newsgroups are not part of the original Usenet but originate from other groups and networks, although all are actually read by the same newsreader software making the distinction somewhat academic (most of the "alt" newsgroups would fall into this category for example).

They are even talking about me on Usenet!

```
─                               MS-DOS Prompt                        ▼ ▲
Wed, 24 Aug 1994 08:38:       alt.fan.wavey.davey       Article:  1 of  2
Subject: Well, I'll go to the foot of our stairs...          13 /  22 lines
From: hirez@epinet.demon.co.uk (Note brains at Bongo Jim and his peppery pen

Ha! Fame and fortune, eh?

What the hell. Couldn't happen to a stranger bloke... >B-)


John 'HiRez' Hawkes-Reed.
"Alleged witty comment."





  ESC=select thread   TAB=next  ENTER=next article  F1 or 'h'=help   [SPACE]
```

Naming Newsgroups

Newsgroups are organised in a hierarchical manner, and after removing the dictionary from my throat I can tell you that this simply means they are named according to an ordered structure. Because there are so many newsgroups they need to be named in such a way that they are easily

All you need to know about the Internet

distinguishable from each other, and easily accessible to the user (although sadly it sometimes seems the opposite is true). Pretty important when you consider that there are, at the time of writing, in excess of 7,000 newsgroups out there and this figure grows all the time. Each group name comprises of a topic and various sub-topics, and all the topics are abbreviated for added confusion. The main topics that you will come across, remember these form the first part of the newsgroup name, are as follows:

alt	Alternative newsgroups, covering a wide variety of subject matter. Some of these newsgroups will be rather offensive to many people, and can include dubious subject matter.
bionet	Newsgroups of interest to Biologists.
bit	BITNET listserv mailing list redistribution.
biz	For product announcements and so on.
clari	A commercial news service, ClariNet.
comp	Discussion and information relating to computers.
de	German language groups.
fj	Japanese language groups.
gnu	The Free Software Federation GNU project.
hepnet	High Energy Physics researchers group (sounds like an odd type of dance music fanatic to me!).
ieee	The Institute of Electrical and Electronics Engineers.
inet	Another method of distributing high volume groups, the "inet" prefix being used to help distinguish from the normally distributed group.
info	University of Illinois mailing list redistribution.
k12	Subjects of interest to teachers of children up to the age of 12 (the children not the teachers that is).
misc	Everything that doesn't fit anywhere else, I guess.
news	Discussion and announcements about Usenet.
rec	Recreational matters, hobbies etc.
relcom	Russian language groups.
sci	Newsgroups that discuss the sciences, funnily enough.
soc	Social matters, psychology, sociology etc.
talk	Chatter and debate, sometimes very strange indeed!
u3b	AT&T 3B computer users (it's OK, I'm as confused as you).
vmsnet	For all DEC VAX/VMS users out there.

The newsgroup name will also have at least one subtopic – some have many subtopics – to further help in identifying its subject matter. Each part of a group name is separated by a period "." which is spoken as "dot" when naming a newsgroup. As an example a newsgroup that discusses palmtop computing is called "comp.sys.palmtops", which expands to computers, systems, palmtops. The whole naming structure does make a lot of sense when you understand the basic components, and most of the subtopic abbreviations are fairly obvious if you give them just a little thought.

MAKE A NOTE!

Some newsgroups are "moderated", which means that you post messages through the group moderator rather than directly to the group itself. The moderator then decides what messages are actually posted within the group, and which are not.

This may seem like petty censorship, but some newsgroups like to keep the subject matter to a clearly defined path and this can be the only way of actually achieving that. In practise there are not too many moderated newsgroups that work very well, mainly due to the burden the job places on the moderator, especially if the newsgroup is at all busy.

Choosing Usenet Newsgroups the easy way, with Ameol on Cix.

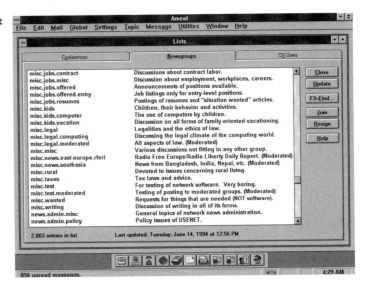

It is quite possible to start your own Usenet Newsgroup, but only if it is felt that the subject matter warrants it. You would have to post a request to create a newsgroup on Usenet itself, and if enough yes votes come in for it then eventually it will appear and be announced in news.news.announcements. For all the gory details on this process I suggest you have a long read of the articles posted in the news.group newsgroup (try saying that with your teeth out).

You may be wondering where to go first as a new user looking at the overwhelming list of newsgroups available, and I don't blame you. I would strongly recommend that all new users take the time involved to read through the articles in the news.announce.newusers newsgroup, as it is there especially to help you get to grips with Usenet. If it was good enough for me, etc. etc.

Netiquette, FAQs, and censorship

Netiquette is a pretty important thing as far as Usenet is concerned – say the wrong thing in the wrong place at the wrong time and be prepared to pay the penalty. You will generally find a FAQ file in most newsgroups – this answers Frequently Asked Questions and will help you to see what sort of behaviour is expected of you within that particular newsgroup. All groups are different, and what is acceptable behaviour in one is seen as an executable offence in another. Let's face it, with the millions of people out there using Usenet you are going to upset someone, sometime. When you do, expect to get flamed.

A flame is just an abusive message, the on-line equivalent to a tantrum or rant, and they are generally, but not always, confined to email.

Wavey's very brief guide to Usenetiquette

And this really is only a skimming the surface exercise, but if you follow these guidelines you should be in a fairly flame free zone.

1)   Read the FAQ for a newsgroup BEFORE you start posting to it.

2)   Don't cross-post to multiple newsgroups unless there is a very good reason for doing so. Even if there is, don't do it too often!

3)   The careful use of a smiley or two can help you convey the intended tone of a posting. However, don't litter your postings with them or they lose all effect and just become bloody annoying little creatures that you want to use a pump action shotgun on (OK I'm calm now).

4)   Don't post long rambling messages when a brief one will do.

5)   Don't quote more than you have to (I wish more people would take note of this) as a 200 line quote followed by a short "I agree" is really a very bad show. Quoting a previous message can be very helpful, just don't overdo it.

6)   Don't post messages which have line lengths exceeding 80 characters. Remember that there are people out there reading your message on all kinds of platform, cater for the lowest common denominator and you won't go far wrong.

7)   Select your newsgroups carefully – don't post a question about bicycles in the computer sciences newsgroups.

8)   Limit your signature to something sensible, say no more than 5 or 6 lines. Don't have a screen full of ASCII graphics in your sig, no matter how pretty or impressive they are. I can assure you it will soon become very boring and very annoying. Wear asbestos underwear if you choose to ignore this advice.

9)   Don't flame someone in a newsgroup. Use email, unless the newsgroup is specifically for flaming of course.

10) Don't shout more than you have to, typing in upper case IS THE ON-LINE EQUIVALENT TO SHOUTING AND VERY HARD ON THE EYES. See what I mean...?

Just a small selection of some of the more, er, unsavoury Newsgroups that exist on Usenet. The groups on the right hand side of the screen are the ones I'm subscribed to, by the way, and are not at all unsavoury. Apart from alt.fan.wavey.davey, maybe.

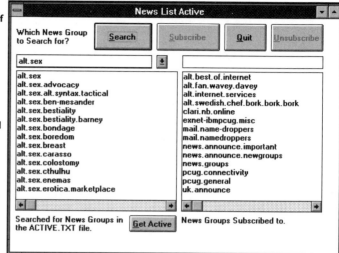

I mentioned earlier that not all Internet service providers offer a full news feed, and there is a reason for this. There are a number of Usenet newsgroups which many people would find offensive, and some providers choose not to make these available at all. These groups are the ones that contain pornographic material, much of which is certainly illegal in the UK and some of which is grossly offensive. However, the numbers of newsgroups carrying such material is absolutely minuscule in the scheme of things, and if you don't like it you don't have to look at it! I'm certainly not going to get involved in the computer pornography debate in this book, I'm sure you can read all about it in many other places. Remember that the overwhelming majority of Usenet postings are not obscene or offensive, they are above all else constructive and useful to an amazingly large number of regular readers.

Chapter 18

Wavey Davey's Useful Usenet

Newsgroup Directory

So you can get a better idea of the newsgroups available, I have put together directory of some of the many newsgroups available at the time of writing. The directory is sorted alphabetically within newsgroup type, and includes a very brief description of the subjects covered in each newsgroup. Please bear in mind that no printed directory can ever hope to be complete, as new newsgroups are being created weekly – this is an area where you can only be up to date if you are on-line! For this reason, and the small matter of available space, this directory does not even attempt to be comprehensive, however I hope it will serve its purpose and help you get a toe in the water by showing you just some of the myriad of topics that are covered.

NEWSGROUP	DESCRIPTION
The alt groups	
alt.3d	3D Imaging
alt.abuse.recovery	Helping abuse victims
alt.activism	A place for activists
alt.adoption	Adoption issues
alt.alien.visitors	They're here!
alt.angst	An anxiety newsgroup
alt.answers	A moderated answers group
alt.aquaria	Fishkeeping as a hobby
alt.archery	Arrow arrow
alt.architecture	Building design etc.
alt.asian-movies	Films from Asia
alt.astrology	Astrological discussion
alt.barney.dinosaur.die.die.die	For Barney haters
alt.bbs	Comms and BBSs
alt.bbs.internet	Internet connected bbs's
alt.beer	Mine's a pint please
alt.best.of.internet	A selection of classics
alt.binaries.multimedia	Multimedia files
alt.binaries.pictures	Gigabytes of images
alt.binaries.pictures.erotica	Pornographic images

alt.binaries.sounds.music	Musical samples
alt.cad	Computer Aided Design
alt.cascade	For owners of big hard disks
alt.cd-rom	CD ROM discussion
alt.censorship	Debate about censorship
alt.cereal	What's your favourite?
alt.comedy.british	UK humour
alt.conspiracy	All the theories you want
alt.cows.moo.moo.moo	For everything bovine
alt.cult-movies	For cult movie fans
alt.culture.internet	What makes Netters tick
alt.cyberpunk	The cyberpunk phenomena
alt.cyberspace	Ditto, cyberspace
alt.devilbunnies	Them darn rabbits!
alt.dreams	Make sense of dreams, or not
alt.drugs	Recreational pharmaceuticals
alt.elvis.king	Dead but not forgotten
alt.fan.*	Newsgroups for fans of just about anyone and anything. Far too many to list here!
alt.fan.wavey.davey	Yep, a newsgroup about me!
alt.flame	The place to flame people
alt.gopher	Serious Gopher discussion
alt.gothic	For Goths everywhere
alt.guitar	Strummers unite
alt.horror	The horror film genre
alt.hotrod	Fast cars
alt.image.medical	Medical image exchange
alt.irc	All about Internet Relay Chat
alt.lang.basic	Everyone's favourite language
alt.magic	Is Paul Daniels on-line?
alt.magick	For real magic!
alt.meditation	Meditation related debate
alt.missing-kids	Helping to find missing kids
alt.msdos.programmer	For the serious msdos techie
alt.music.*	Lots of music related groups
alt.out-of-body	Out of body experiences

All you need to know about the Internet

alt.pagan	Pagan beliefs and practises
alt.pantyhose	For the stocking fancier!
alt.party	An on-line party
alt.personals	For the terminally sad
alt.politics.*	Long list of newsgroups that are into politics of every colour and then some.
alt.punk	For punk rockers everywhere
alt.quotations	Quotes on-line
alt.rock-n-roll.*	Various groups covering all aspects of rock-n-roll, from music to partying.
alt.security	Computer security issues
alt.sex.*	A number of newsgroups which cover every aspect of sex and sexuality, on the whole most of these group contain material that many would consider offensive
alt.slack	The Church of the Subgenius
alt.sports.*	Every kind of sport has a newsgroup of its own
alt.startrek.creative	Well, there had to be really
alt.swedish.chef.bork.bork.bork	Talk like the Muppet chef!
alt.tv.*	Groups covering lots of tv shows, mainly American
alt.wedding	A getting hitched group
alt.wired	Discuss Wired magazine

The bionet groups

bionet.announce	Moderated announcements
bionet.biology.tropical	Topical tropical biology
bionet.general	General biology discussion
bionet.immunology	Immunology research
bionet.jobs	Science related vacancies
bionet.plants	Plant biology
bionet.software	Biological software info
bionet.virology	Viruses, real ones!

The bit groups

bit.general	General Bitnet discussion
bit.listserv.music	All types of music
bit.listserv.bitnews	Bitnet news
bit.listserv.buslib-l	Business libraries list
bit.listserv.cinema-l	Discussion on cinema
bit.listserv.dbase-l	For dBASE IV users
bit.listserv.deaf-l	Mailing list for deaf people
bit.listserv.euearn-l	Computing in Eastern Europe
bit.listserv.frac-l	Fractals discussion
bit.listserv.games-l	Computer games
bit.listserv.gaynet	GayNet discussion
bit.listserv.ibm-main	IBM mainframes
bit.listserv.ioob-l	Industrial psychology
bit.listserv.l-hcap	Disability issues
bit.listserv.license	Software licensing
bit.listserv.lstsrv-l	Listserv discussion
bit.listserv.next-l	NeXT computers
bit.listserv.novell	Novell LAN
bit.listserv.os2-l	OS/2 debate
bit.listserv.postcard	Postcard collectors
bit.listserv.s-comput	Super Computing
bit.listserv.techwr-l	Technical writing
bit.listserv.valert-l	Virus alert list
bit.listserv.vmslsv-l	VAX/VMS discussion
bit.listserv.win3-l	Windows 3 debate
bit.listserv.word-mac	Word processing on the Mac
bit.listserv.word-pc	Word processing on the PC

The biz groups

biz.books.technical	Publishers adverts and info
biz.clarinet	ClariNet announcements
biz.comp.hardware	Commercial hardware posts
biz.comp.software	Commercial software posts
biz.misc	Miscellaneous commercial postings

All you need to know about the Internet

biz.next.newprod	NeXT announcements
biz.sco.	general SCO products forum
biz.stolen	Stolen equipment postings

The clari groups

clari.biz.courts	Legal matters
clari.biz.features	Business stories
clari.biz.finance	Financial matters
clari.biz.market	Stock market news
clari.local.*	News local to specified US States
clari.net.newusers	For new ClariNet users
clari.net.talk	General chatter
clari.news.books	Books and publishing
clari.news.europe	European related news items
clari.news.flash	Important news flashes

The comp groups

comp.ai	Artificial intelligence
comp.apps.spreadsheets	Various spreadsheet platforms
comp.arch	Computer architecture
comp.archives	Public access archives
comp.bbs.misc	Bulletin Boards discussed
comp.benchmarks	Benchmarking techniques
comp.binaries.*	Encoded binary files for most popular platforms and operating systems. These are not pirate programs, but PD and Shareware programs.
comp.client-server	Client/Server related matters
comp.cog-eng	Cognitive engineering
comp.compilers	Computer compilers discussed
comp.compression	Data compression methods
comp.databases	Databases of all types
comp.doc	PD documentation archive
comp.dsp	Digital Signal Processing
comp.edu	Computer science in education

comp.fonts	Fonts discussion
comp.graphics	Computer graphics in depth
comp.groupware	Hardware and software for shared environments
comp.infosystems	Information systems
comp.lang.*	Just about every computer language has a group here for its followers and detractors to participate in
comp.mail.*	Various groups discussing different aspects of email
comp.multimedia	All things MM
comp.object	Object Oriented programming
comp.org.*	Various computer related organisations and societies have their own discussion groups
comp.os.*	Every possible operating system is covered as well
comp.periphs	Computer peripherals
comp.sources.*	Source code for every platform
comp.speech	Speech synthesis research
comp.sys.*	Groups devoted to a specific computer system. There are a great number of comp.sys groups to choose from
comp.terminals	Terminals galore debated
comp.text	Text processing
comp.unix.*	Various newsgroups which look at all aspects of UNIX
comp.virus issues	Computer virus and security related
comp.windows.*	Groups dealing with various MS Windows related topics

The gnu groups

gnu.announce	Gnu project announcements
gnu.chess	Gnu Chess announcements

All you need to know about the Internet

gnu.emacs.*	Various groups relating to the Gnu Emacs program
gnu.g++.*	Various groups relating to the Gnu C++ Compiler

The hepnet groups

hepnet.announce	Announcements in general
hepnet.general	General discussion
hepnet.jobs	Situations vacant
hepnet.lang.c++	C++ discussion
hepnet.videoconf	Videoconferencing debate

The ieee groups

ieee.announce	IEEE announcements
ieee.rab.announce	Regional activities
ieee.tab.announce	Technical activities
ieee.tcos	Technical Committee on Operating Systems

The misc groups

misc.consumers	Consumer related news
misc.education	The education system
misc.fitness	Health and beauty
misc.forsale	Classifieds
misc.handicap	Disability issues (moderated)
misc.invest	Investment news
misc.jobs.offered	Situations vacant
misc.kids	All about children
misc.misc	A real mixed bag!
misc.rural	Living in the countryside
misc.writing	For all writers and readers

The news groups

news.admin.policy	Usenet admin policy
news.announce.conferences	Conference announcements
news.announce.important	Important general information
news.announce.newgroups	Announcements of new groups
news.announce.newusers	BEGIN HERE!
news.future	Where is it all heading?
news.groups	Newsgroup discussion
news.misc	Usenet discussion
news.newusers.questions	Everything you need to know

The rec groups

rec.antiques	For antique collectors
rec.aquaria	Fishkeeping
rec.arts.*	Every conceivable branch of the arts, from comics and bonsai through to poems and, of course, Star Trek
rec.audio	Hi-Fi
rec.aviation.*	A collection of groups that are devoted to all things aircraft rec.bicycles.misc Cycling
rec.birds	Ornithology
rec.boats	A life on the ocean wave
rec.collecting	Collectors of all kinds
rec.equestrian	For horsey types
rec.gambling	Games of chance
rec.games.*	A huge lists of groups which cover all aspects of games from chess to muds
rec.guns	Only in America, huh?
rec.heraldry	Coats of Arms and so on
rec.humour	Well, you have to laugh
rec.kites	Let's go fly a kite...
rec.motorcycles	For bikers everywhere
rec.music.*	Every taste in music is catered for in one of these groups

rec.pets	For pet lovers and haters
rec.scouting	Scouts worldwide
rec.sport.*	Every sport possible
rec.travel	For world-wide travellers
rec.video	Video and video components
rec.windsurfing	Get that virtual board out

The sci groups

sci.aeronautics	Aeronautics and related stuff
sci.anthropology	The study of mankind
sci.aquaria	Fishkeeping from a scientific perspective this time
sci.archaeology	For everything archaeological
sci.chem	Chemistry related topics
sci.classics	The classics, from any field
sci.cryonics	Suspended animation
sci.crypt	Data encryption
sci.econ	The science of economics
sci.edu	The science of education
sci.engr	Engineering debate
sci.logic	All aspects of logic
sci.med	Medicine
sci.military	The military aspects of science
sci.physics	The science of physics
sci.polymers	Polymers, what else?
sci.research	Scientific research
sci.skeptics	For scientific skeptics
sci.space	To boldly go where....
sci.virtual-worlds	Virtual Reality

The soc groups

soc.bi	Bisexuality
soc.college	College life
soc.culure.*	Various groups discussing all aspects of different cultures world-wide

soc.feminism	Feminist issues debated
soc.history	All things historical
soc.men	Men talk
soc.motss	Members Of The Same Sex
soc.penpals	Search the nets for friends
soc.rights.human	Human rights
soc.roots	Family tree type stuff
soc.women	Women's talk

The talk groups

talk.abortion	Abortion debated
talk.bizarre	Very off the wall and distinctly odd discussion.
talk.origins	Evolution or Creationism?
talk.politics.*	Various very noisy groups
talk.rape	Rape issues debated
talk.rumours	Did you hear about…

The vmsnet groups

vmsnet.announce	General announcements
vmsnet.decus.journal	The DECUServe Journal
vmsnet.employment	Situations vacant
vmsnet.misc	General VMA related items
vmsnet.networks.*	Various VMS network related topics
vmsnet.sources	Source code postings vmsnet.vms-posix
	VMS POSIX discussion group

Chapter 19

Internet Relay Chat

Nobody calls it Internet Relay Chat, so from now on we shall use the accepted acronym of IRC – that's much easier isn't it? Developed by Jarkko Oikarinen from Finland, who can often be seen using his baby under the nickname of "wiz", IRC enables you to talk to other Internet users in real time, all around the globe. Although the number of users of IRC is small when compared with the millions of people who are actually connected to the Internet, it is still fairly significant. Currently there are in excess of 150 IRC servers, and as many as 4,000 or so simultaneous users.

Not just something to do when you get back from the pub, IRC has had its moments in the recent past. For example, during the Gulf War hundreds of users got together on a single IRC channel to listen to reports of the bombings from users logging in from Iraq. During the Russian coup against Yeltsin in 1993 IRC users in Moscow gave "as it happened" reports to people all over the world.

IRC client at Cix

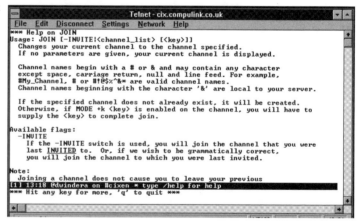

MAKE A
NOTE!

IRC users are known by nicknames, usually the same as your login name, and these are unique. You won't be allowed to enter IRC using a nickname that is already spoken for, and will have to keep trying until you find one that is free.

Internet Relay Chat has a structure that is similar to Usenet, but instead of having newsgroups to talk about different subjects IRC has channels. On entering the system you will find yourself in channel 0, the null channel, from there you can choose which channels you want to join. There are four types of channel available on IRC, each with differing levels of privacy and security.

○ **Channels 1 - 999** are known as public channels. Every user of these channels can see every other user logged on, and contribute to conversations as they please.

○ **Channels from 1000 on** are known as "secret" channels, and although other users can see that you are connected to the IRC system they cannot tell which channel you are using – unless, of course, they are using that channel as well!

○ **Channels with a negative number** are designated as "hidden" channels, and they hide the user from all others. Nobody can see that you are using IRC while you use these channels, apart from the people in the channel with you.

IRC client running at Delphi.

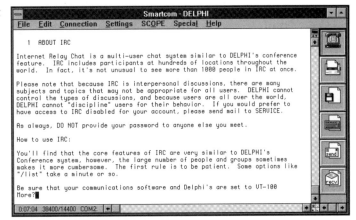

String channels offer the ultimate in IRC security. They are anonymous, strictly moderated, and you can only join them by invitation. A string channel is denoted by a prefix of + before the channel number. However, don't think this means your conversations are totally secure here, as any IRC Administrator could log and read any messages that pass through its server!

More and more Service Providers now have IRC clients that you can use. To see if yours does just type irc and see if you get any response. If you don't have access to an IRC client through your service provider, or set up an IRC client on your own computer, then you will find it hard to get connected any other way. Vast numbers of IRC servers have closed down over the last few months, and it is very hard to find places to telnet to that will accept anonymous users. However, at the time of writing I was able to find two public IRC servers that were still running, although I can give no guarantees they will still be when you try them! Anyway, here are the URLs:

`telnet://sci.dixie.edu 6677`

`telnet://vinson.ecn.uoknor.edu 6677`

IRC from a public access server.

IRC commands

Once you're connected to IRC there are a number of commands that you will need to get to grips with. While these can seem somewhat confusing to start with, even for the Internet veterans out there who may not have stumbled across IRC yet, it all makes sense pretty quickly. Especially if you use Wavey Daveys Patent IRC Command Reference.

The most useful command you can use initially is the first on this list. Try it, go on...

/help	This gives you lots of useful information about using IRC
/admin	Returns administrative information about a specified IRC server (wow, that's a really interesting one Wavey!)
/away	Lets you leave a short message which explains your absence should you want to remain connected to IRC but go away and do something else for a while. Especially useful when you need to see a man about a dog!
/channel	Join a specified channel
/clear	Clears the terminal screen
/cmdch	Change the command character from / to whatever takes your fancy, if you really don't like that poor little backslash
/describe	Sends information about yourself to either a channel or a specified user
/ignore	Virtual murder! Kills the output from a specified user to you screen, so you don't have to read the rubbish he/she is spouting
/invite	Invite a specified user to join you in any specified channel
/join	Join a specified channel
/kick	Forcibly remove a specified user from the current channel
/lastlog	Display the most recent messages from within the current channel. The number of entries to show can be specified as an argument
/leave	Exit from a channel
/links	Lists currently active IRC servers
/list	Lists all the active public channels, and includes details about the number of users and associated topics
/me	Sends information about yourself to a channel, a sort of mini resume
/msg	Allows you to send a single private message to a specified user
/nick	Changes your nickname to something else
/notify	Gives you information as specified users enter or exit the IRC system

/**query**	You can use this command to establish a private conversation outside of the usual channel structure. This works by two users issuing the command and each specifying the other user, for example if I issue a /query noddy command and noddy issues a /query wavey command, we will be in a private communications channel between just the two of us. Issuing the /query command again, but with no arguments, will exit the private channel
/**signoff**	Finish your session and leave IRC
/**users**	Returns a list of all users logged on to a specified host server, the default being the current server
/**who**	Tells you who is currently using IRC, but the information returned depends on what channels people are using (as explained previously)
/**whois**	Gives you information about a specific user
/**whowas**	Gives you information about a specific user who has just left the system, or changed nickname.

Chapter 20

Mailing lists

Mailing lists perform a similar function to Usenet Newsgroups, and to the type of forums and conferences you might find on the big commercial on-line systems. Indeed, many mailing lists are the same as Usenet Newsgroups, they are archived versions made available to all subscribers, and with the added advantage of having much of the wibble filtered out. The main differences being that anyone who has an Internet accessible email address can participate in mailing lists. The lists offer group discussion on specific subjects, some technical, some social, many off the wall. If you can cope with email then you can use a mailing list with ease, all you do is send a mail message to the specified address and it will then get distributed, by email, to everyone else on the list. Pretty simple stuff, but then the best ideas always are.

Suscription costs nothing

There are two main types of mailing list, and both of them will cost you no more than a bit of time and some hard disk space.

The human touch

First, you may want to join a mailing list that is maintained manually, that is a list that is actually managed by a human being (remember them?) rather than a computer process. This type of mailing list is starting to lose favour to LISTSERV distributed ones as time progresses, but there are still thousands of them around and I have a sneaking feeling there always will be. You can identify the human touch by the fact that the subscription address will almost always take the form of the list name with a suffix of '-request attached'. For example, if you are a keen Harley Davidson motorbike enthusiast (why didn't I just say "an American biker"?) you may be interested in a mailing list called, simply, "harley". To subscribe to this list you would need to send Email asking so to do, to "**harley-request@thinkage.com**". If you sent your subscription request to "**harley@thinkage.com**" it would get seen by everybody who is on the distribution list, and you be a source of endless amusement for the big butch bikers who no doubt hang around in such a place.

Because these types of mailing list are maintained by a real live human bean, you don't need to follow a particular format for your subscription request. However, it would be good manners to keep the request short

and to the point, and ensuring you include your real name. An example of the kind of subscription request I'd be happy to receive would be:

List: Teapots

Please subscribe me to the Teapots mailing list. My full name is Davey Archibald Aardvark Winder.

To serve them all my days

You are ever increasingly likely to come across mailing lists that are maintained and managed without the need for those old fashioned human things to get involved too much. These are known by the common name of LISTSERV. In fact, LISTSERV is the name of the program that actually deals with the mailing list subscriptions, resignations, distribution and so on. This type of list has become very popular, mainly because it involves a lot less work (in fact none at all unless the list is moderated, and then it's just a matter of someone approving (or not) the subscription applications).

Subscribing to a Mailing List is easy, here's a real life example.

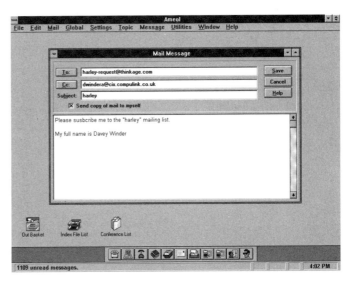

All you need to know about the Internet

You can easily tell if a mailing list is of the LISTSERV genre, because you will have to send your subscription request to a LISTSERV address. Each LISTSERV site may well distribute many different mailing lists, so you need to ensure that you specify which list you are wanting to join. The subscription request must follow a specific format, with the following text in the body of the message you send:

`sub <list> <your name>`

So if I wanted to subscribe to a mailing list called "BongoBongo" I would use the format:

`sub BongoBongo Davey Norbert Ramsbottom Winder`

Say that this mailing list was one of the ones that is distrbuted at a LISTSERV at wavey.demon.co.uk, then my subscription request would be Emailed to:

`listserv@wavey.demon.co.uk`

(And for the hard of thinking, this example has been totally fabricated by myself. If you really want to join a mailing list called BongoBongo you'll have to go elsewhere – how about a nice doctor for starters?)

 If you want to get yourself off of a LISTSERV mailing list, then you need to send email to the same LISTSERV address that you used to subscribe in the first place, with the following text in the message:

signoff <list>

If you want to find out what all the LISTSERV mailing lists are, and there are more than 4000 of them, then you can get this information by sending an email message to:

`listserv@bitnic.educom.edu`

With a body text of:

```
list global
```

But do be warned by Wavey, even though the descriptions for each list are short, the whole list itself is enormous!

Alternatively you could send email to:

listserv@vm1.nodak.edu

With a body text of:

GET NEWLIST WOUTERS

For a copy of the "How To Find An Interesting Mailing List" file by Arno Wouters.

Finally, if you prefer to FTP these things, then try

ftp.nisc.sri.com

And look in the path of /netfind/interest-groups for a list of mailing lists.

MAKE A
NOTE!

You may also come across other mailing list distribution methods, all of them work in much the same way but you will need to follow whatever instructions are given to ensure you are doing things correctly. Examples of some of these alternative distribution methods include: Majordomo, Almanac, Mailbase, and Mailserv.

Chapter 21

Wavey Davey's Mad Mailing List Directory

There really are thousands of Mailing Lists, of one type or another, and trying to list them all would result in three things:

1)   A very long list

2)   A very boring list

3)   A very bored Wavey

Therefore, what I have attempted to do in compiling the Wavey Davey Mailing List Directory is to provide as diverse, interesting, and useful a group of lists as I can. Hopefully you will find something of interest, whether you are just idly browsing or have a particular subject matter you want to find out about. You will also notice I have abandoned the URLs that appear in all the other resource directories in this book. This is because I simply believe that the URL format doesn't lend itself particularly well to Mailing Lists!

So without further ado, on with the directory!

Subject	Act-Up
List Name	act-up
Contact Address	`act-up-request@world.std.com`
Description	Discussion of the work of the various Act-Up groups world-wide. Act-Up looks at the politics of AIDS and AIDS related health care.

Subject	AIDS
List Name	aids
Contact Address	`aids-request@cs.ucla.edu`
Description	Information and discussion relating to all aspects of Acquired Immune Deficiency Syndrome.

Subject	AMOS
List Name	amos
Contact Address	`subscribe@xamiga.linet.org`
Description	Not for discussion of Emmerdale Farm characters, but rather the popular Amiga programming language, AMOS.

Subject	Argentina
List Name	argentina
Contact Address	`argentina-request@ois.db.toronto.edu`
Description	Anything and everything Argentina. Helps if you can speak, or at least read, Spanish.

Subject	Art of Noise
List Name	aon
Contact Address	`aon-request@polyslo.csc.CalPoly.edu`
Description	A discussion come fan club for the Art of Noise band. Probably best not to mention Tom Jones too often here though...

Subject	Ayurveda
List Name	ayurveda
Contact Address	`ayurveda-request@netcom.com`
Description	Ayurveda is the ancient science of life.

Subject	Ballooning
List Name	balloon
Contact Address	`balloon-request@lut.ac.uk`
Description	If you have any interest in any type of ballooning this is the place to let off some hot air about it.

Subject	Ballroom Dancing
List Name	ballroom
Contact Address	`ballroom-request@athena.mit.edu`
Description	The ballroom dancing discussion area. Information on clubs, music and steps is exchanged here.

Subject	Blindness
List Name	BlindNws
Contact Address	`listserv@vm1.nodak.edu`
Description	The Blind News Digest deals with all aspects of vision impairment and blindness

Subject	Bonsai Trees
List Name	bonsai
Contact Address	`listserv@cms.cc.wayne.edu`
Description	For anyone who thinks small is best.

Subject	Caving
List Name	cavers
Contact Address	`cavers-request@clsi.bu.edu`
Description	The mailing list for anyone interested in exploring caves, and yes, this means YOU Toby!

Subject	Chess List
List Name	chessnews
Contact Address	`chessnews-request@tssi.com`
Description	This is a copy of the Usenet "rec.games,chess" newsgroup, which has a bi-directional mailing facility as a feature.

Subject	Comics
List Name	comix
Contact Address	`comix-request@world.std.com`
Description	For readers and collectors of non mainstream comics.

Subject	Dark Side of the Net
List Name	dark side of the net
Contact Address	`carriec@eskimo.com`
Description	For all things Gothic, Horror, Vampire, Occult

Subject	Depeche Mode
List Name	bong
Contact Address	`bong-request@lestat.compaq.com`
Description	For fans of Depeche Mode everywhere, I wonder if they could tell me why the guy keeps on singing after he has said "words are so very unnecessary" in Enjoy The Silence?

Subject	Deviants
List Name	deviants
Contact Address	`deviants-request@csv.warwick.ac.uk`
Description	For deviants the world over, especially those who follow the teachings of the Great Wok!

Subject	Dinosaurs
List Name	dinosaur
Contact Address	`dinosaur_request@ctsx.celtech.com`
Description	The dinosaur discussion group no less. I wonder if you can talk about Barney here?

Subject	Downs Syndrome
List Name	downs-syndrome
Contact Address	`listserv@vm1.nodak.edu`
Description	Discussion and support forum regarding Downs Syndrome

Subject	Emplant Macintosh Emulator
List Name	emplant
Contact Address	`subscribe@xamiga.linet.org`
Description	Information about the "Emplant" Macintosh emulator for the Amiga computer.

Subject	Exotic Cars
List Name	exotic-cars
Contact Address	`exotic-cars-request@sol.asl.hitachi.com`
Description	If you are a fan of all those ultra expensive and/or ultra rare cars, here is the place you can talk about them with fellow enthusiasts. All aspects including driving, maintenance, design.

Subject	Feminine issues
List Name	femail
Contact Address	`femail-request@lucerne.eng.sun.com`
Description	A list intended to provide a forum for the discussion of issues of interest to women, in a friendly atmosphere. Both men and women can participate, but the list is Moderated and there are joining requirements.

Subject	Ferrets
List Name	ferret
Contact Address	`request@ferret.ocunix.on.ca`
Description	Stick 'em down your trousers or just keep them in a cage. Whatever your interest in ferrets, don't miss out on this mailing list.

Subject	Fiction Writers
List Name	fiction-writers
Contact Address	`writers-request@studguppy.lanl.gov`
Description	The Fiction Writers Group is a forum for both sharing information on fiction writing between the professional and wannabee fiction writer, and an environment where work can be made available for criticism and review. All areas of fiction are catered for, although the emphasis at present does seem to be on Science Fiction for some strange reason.

Subject	Film Making
List Name	filmmakers
Contact Address	`filmmakers-request@grissom.larc.nasa.gov`
Description	This list is all about movie making, covering all aspects but with an emphasis on the technical side of things.

Subject	Football
List Name	european review
Contact Address	`s947607@umslvma.umsl.edu`
Description	A newsletter all about football in Europe. Here we go, here we go, here we… or perhaps not.

Subject	Games Reviews
List Name	digital-games
Contact Address	`digital-games-request@intuitive.com`
Description	Computer games reviews, written by computer games enthusiasts

Subject	Gay Issues
List Name	GayNet
Contact Address	`majordomo@queernet.org`
Description	A mailing list for gays, lesbians, and bisexuals. There is an emphasis on the Stateside gay community though

Subject	Gender
List Name	gender
Contact Address	`ericg@indiana.edu`
Description	A list created to explore gender issues, an open minded forum for discussing gender stereotyping vs individuality.

Subject	Hang Gliding
List Name	hang gliding
Contact Address	`hang-gliding-request@virginia.edu`
Description	Everything to do with the sport of hang gliding.

All you need to know about the Internet **.net** the internet magazine

Subject   Harley Davidson
List Name   harley
Contact Address   `harley-request@thinkage.com`
Description   For Hog fans everywhere. Just about everything even
                   remotely connected to Harleys is talked about here.
                   Jump on and ride free.

Subject   Hockey
List Name   uk-hockey
Contact Address   `uk-hockey-request@uk.ac.hw.cs`
Description   The mailing list to join if you want to know about, or
                   are a great fan of, ice hockey in the UK. Includes
                   league tables, results, news, and gossip.

Subject   Horse Racing
List Name   derby
Contact Address   `derby-request@ekrl.com`
Description   A list that discusses all aspect of horse racing.

Subject   INXS
List Name   INXS
Contact Address   `INXS-list-request@iastate.edu`
Description   A mailing list devoted to the rock group INXS.

Subject   Internet Relay Chat
List Name   irchat
Contact Address   `irchat-request@cc.tut.fi`
Description   This, oddly enough, is where you can chat about
                   Internet Relay Chat (IRC). Damn funny idea, why not
                   chat on IRC? That's what it's for, after all.

Subject   Jewish
List Name   jewish
Contact Address   `avi_feldblum@att.com`
Description   A non abusive forum for debate on all issues Jewish.
                   There is an emphasis on Jewish law.

Subject	Killifish
List Name	killie
Contact Address	`killie-request@chama.unm.edu`
Description	A list that discusses killifish (that's the family cyprinodontidae for all the ichthyologists reading this). I think it's a crying shame that the Elasmobranchii haven't got a mailing list of their own though (and that's sharks and rays for all the non-ichthyologists reading this).

Subject	Law
List Name	uklegal
Contact Address	`lsg001@uk.ac.coventry.cck`
Description	A mailing list that covers all aspects of United Kingdon law

Subject	Lute
List Name	lute
Contact Address	`lute-request@sunapee.dartmouth.edu`
Description	For all (all, now do be serious, possibly the one who may be reading this) lute players and lute music researchers.

Subject	LOGO
List Name	logo-friends
Contact Address	`logo-friends-request@aiai.ed.ac.uk`
Description	For fans of the LOGO computer language.

Subject	Magic
List Name	magic
Contact Address	`magic-request@crdgw1.ge.com`
Description	You're going to like this, not a lot! Yes, it's the pull a rabbit out of the hat brigade and they are on the Net! Aaaaarrgghh! Run for the hills, there is no escape.

Subject	Mensa
List Name	mensatalk
Contact Address	`mensatalk-request@psg.com`
Description	For members of Mensa, the awfully clever chaps society, to get together and talk about whatever eggheads talk about.

Subject	Nordic Skiing
List Name	nordic-skiing
Contact Address	`nordic-ski-request@graphics.cornell.edu`
Description	This list is for all types of Nordic skiing sports, such as cross country, biathlon, ski jumping, and ski-orienteering.

Subject	Oyster Band
List Name	oysters
Contact Address	`oysters-request@blowfish.taligent.com`
Description	The fan conference of the Oyster Band, rather than a place where a band of oysters get together for a chinwag (hey, do oysters have chins? How about a mollusc wag…)

Subject	Pagans
List Name	pagan
Contact Address	`request@drycas.club.cc.cmu.edu`
Description	A mailing list that discusses all aspects of Paganism

Subject	Pen Pals
List Name	pen-pals
Contact Address	`pen-pals-request@mainstream.com`
Description	A mailing list with a difference! This one is to help kids from around the world find electronic pen pals. The list is moderated so as to stop any abuse of its aims.

Subject	Philip K Dick
List Name	pkd-list
Contact Address	`pkd-list-request@wang.com`
Description	For fans of the cult science fiction writer, Philip K Dick.

Subject	Queen
List Name	queen
Contact Address	`com@spacsun.rice.edu`
Description	For fans of Queen and the late great Freddie Mercury. Don't join this list if all you want to know is the price of admission to Buckingham Palace.

Subject	Rolling Stones
List Name	undercover
Contact Address	`undercover-request@¬` `snowhite.cis.uoguelph.ca`
Description	For fans of the Rolling Stones, wherever you may be. If you can't get no satisfaction anywhere else then try this list!

Subject	Satnews
List Name	satnews
Contact Address	`listserv@orbital.demon.co.uk`
Description	The mailing list for the Satnews publication, which looks at the world-wide satellite television industry.

Subject	Scottish Country Dancing
List Name	strathspey
Contact Address	`strathspey-request@math.uni-frankfurt.de`
Description	For anyone interested in Scottish country dancing

Subject	SupraFAX Modems
List Name	suprafax
Contact Address	`subscribe@xamiga.linet.org`
Description	For owners of SupraFAX V32bis modems, especially those who have experienced difficulties with this particular model.

Subject	Twins
List Name	twins
Contact Address	`owner-twins@athena.mit.edu`
Description	Yes not one, but two of the little, er, lovely creatures. If you've got twins you'll probably need the support this group offers!

Subject	Volvo
List Name	volvo
Contact Address	`volvo-net-request@me.rochester.edu`
Description	Those damn Volvo drivers get everywhere, don't they?

Subject	Windsurfing
List Name	windsurfing
Contact Address	`windsurfing-request@gcm.com`
Description	A mailing list for all boardsailors.

Subject	Yello
List Name	yello
Contact Address	`yello-request@polyslo.calpoly.edu`
Description	A fan list for the band "Yello".

Subject	Zeppelin
List Name	zeppelin
Contact Address	`zeppelin-l@cornell.edu`
Description	This could be your Stairway to Heaven if you are a Led Zeppelin fan.

Chapter 22

Accessing the Internet –

a hands-on look

In this chapter of the book I shall be taking a look at actually using the Internet with some of the many Service Providers available to you. Just because I've left any particular service out doesn't mean it is no good, but rather it means that I don't have the space to go into detail on them all.

I am concentrating on the Service Providers I know, and that I actually use. By doing this I can pass on my hard earned experience to give you a quick-start guide to the various options available. My aim is that by reading through the following sections, you will get an impression of which Service Provider sounds best suited for you personally. I hope that I can give you a good enough "feel" for the systems mentioned so that you will be happy with your choice and will be able to get straight on with the business of using the Internet.

MAKE A NOTE!

I have, purposefully, concentrated on UK Service Providers (although I have included the likes of CompuServe). If you want to read about US based services there are approximately 70 Internet books available that will satisfy you.

Personally, I'm fed up with the total lack of UK coverage and hope that I can redress the balance somewhat with this book. After all, why bother reading about services that it would be totally impractical for you to use? If, like me, you want a Service Provider who understands the UK market, who can cater for your needs, who can help with your technical problems, then read on…

Accessing the Internet with dial-up on-line services

Although Internet access isn't the primary function of any of these systems, it is something that has become a very important part of their development. None of them at the time of writing offer a direct connection to the Internet, so no graphical browsers for World Wide Web or personal domain addresses (you will always be **fredbloggs@the.big.service.co**). The advantages are many, and are looked at in depth for each provider. I personally use all of these services on a very regular basis, daily in fact! You can rest assured that my experience is hard won, so why not take advantage of it and read on if you are thinking of taking the "On-line System" approach to Internetting...

MAKE A
NOTE!

All Service Providers mentioned are listed in alphabetical order within each categories section. In no way does the ordering represent any preference or recommendation on my part.

Access with Cix

The Compulink Information eXchange, or Cix for short (not to be confused with the Commercial Internet Exchange, which is a totally different Cix altogether) provides a "Dial Up" connection to the Internet. This means that whilst Cix have a direct connection to the Internet you as a user do not, you are using their connection. This makes little or no difference to much of what you may get up to on the Internet, but there are some areas where it falls short of a direct or "Dial In" SLIP/PPP connection.

The **CIX** welcome screen.

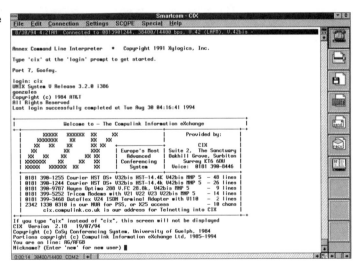

1) Because you are not connected directly to the Internet you don't have your own host domain, but rather are a user at the Cix host domain (i.e. **dwindera@cix.compulink.co.uk**)

2) Transferring files is a two stage process as firstly they have to be downloaded to your Internet directory at Cix, and then downloaded from the Cix computer to your own. While this process is made fairly simple, it does take twice as long as a direct connection to the Net.

3) You cannot use a graphical browser such as Mosaic or Cello to navigate the World Wide Web, instead you must use the character based browser at Cix.

However, there are also a number of advantages to using Cix for Internet access.

1) No hassle in setting up software. It has all been done for you, regardless of your chosen computing platform.

2) You can use an Off Line Reader to perform some of the more common Internet tasks, such as Archie searches and FTP requests.

The **Ameol** off line reader for Cix, showing some of its easy to use Internet access scripts.

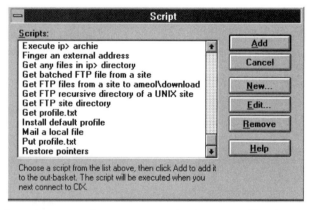

3) You get a value added service, as well as access to the Internet. Cix gives you thousands of conferences to participate in, Gigabytes of files online for you to download, a shopping subsystem, excellent email facilities including internal binary mail transfers, and an efficient technical support service.

4) There is a very active and useful "internet" conference on Cix (moderated by myself and another Internet expert by the name of Steve

Hebditch) where experts will answer your questions, and where users share their experiences of the Net.

The thriving internet conference on Cix has these topics to help you on your way.

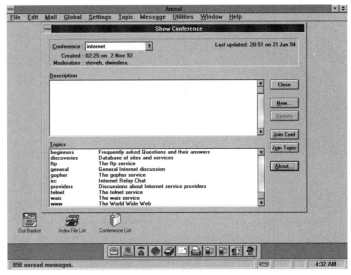

Internet email

Sending email across the Internet is really simple with Cix, you just go to the Mail: prompt as you would to send mail to another Cixen but specify the full email address rather than just a username. For example, if someone was sending me email from within Cix they would send it to:

dwindera

If they were sending email to me at an external Internet address, say my PC User Group address, then they would just add the full address and send it to:

wavey@waveydavey.win-uk.net

If you are using one of the many Off Line Readers for Cix then it becomes even simpler, with the ability to store both internal Cix addresses and external Internet addresses in an Address Book and send your email at the click of a mouse button!

Getting started

The first thing you will need to do to connect to the Internet with Cix is to actually leave the main system and join the Internet subsystem. This is accomplished by simply typing

`go internet`

from the Main: or Read: prompts. Once connected to the Internet subsystem you will be greeted with an ip> prompt. You will also be told that there is some online help available to you. This is in the form of a list of available commands, a list of helpfiles aviable, and help on individual commands.

The on-line help at the Cix Internet Gateway.

The commands available, together with tips on using them, are:

address   This is a very useful command indeed, and one that I'm sure you will find yourself using as much as I do. If you enter a piece of text as an argument, that text being the subject matter that you are interested in, then Cix will return a list of Internet sites which have something to do with that subject. Cix keeps an online database of site information, and usually you can get some idea of a starting place on the Net by using the address command. The one drawback with this command is that the information in the database is limited, and there are times when you will get no results at all, in which case you don't get told as such but just get dumped unceremoniously back at the IP> prompt!

The Cix "address" feature in full flow.

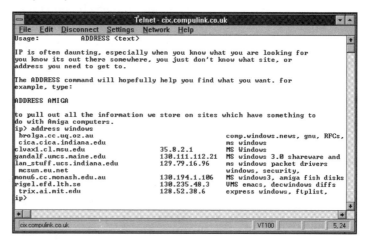

archie

Using the Cix archie client will connect you to the server at **archie.doc.ic.ac.uk** where a database of files available at all anonymous FTP sites is kept. Use archie before using the batchftp command, so you can find out the exact pathname you will require. Archie is real easy to use from Cix, just type:

ARCHIE <filename>

The results of an archie search are stored in your Internet diretory in a file called archie.lis which you can look at by using the view command.

batchftp

This allows a file, or files, to be downloaded by FTP to your Internet directory but as a background process. You tell Cix which files you want to FTP, and where they can be found, and then go and do something else. BatchFTP requests are dealt with every 20 minutes, starting on the hour, so it won't be too long until your files are transferred to your Internet directory, along with a status file which gives full details of all BatchFTP attempts, including any reasons for failure. To use BatchFTP you need to know the exact details of where the file or files you want are stored. You can get this information by using the Archie command as described earlier. If you wanted to FTP the file teapot.gif which you know is stored at **wuarchive.wustl.edu** in the directory **/pub/pictures/misc/teapots**, then to use BatchFTP you would type:

```
BATCHFTP wuarchive.wustl.edu
/pub/pictures/misc/teapot.gif
```

To download the file, and any others you may have requested in a BatchFTP session, you use the BATCHFTP GET command. Typing this command downloads all files which appear in your batchftp.rep file and then deletes them after a successful transfer. If any file doesn't download properly, it gets left in your Internet directory so you can get it later. You can check to see how your FTP request is coming on by using the BATCHFTP STATUS command, which will give basic details of the BatchFTP queue. For a more detailed report on your job status you can use the BATCHFTP LIST command. If you want to stop any of your BatchFTP requests you can issue a BATCHFTP KILL command.

dir   This command will produce a list of the files currently stored in your Cix Internet directory.

dossify   This is, actually, a very handy little command if you are a PC user who is fed up of renaming all those long filenames that you get from an FTP session, so the files conform to the DOS 8.3 naming format. Dossify strips all odd characters from the filename and then automatically converts it to a 8.3 format name for you!

erase   Deletes the specified file from your Internet directory.

finger   Gets information, sometimes, about a specified site or user. To use the finger command type: finger @ <site> or finger <user>@<site> Although currently a tad temperamental, you can let other Internet users finger you as a Cix user by including the following command in your resume, everything after which will be displayed when someone fingers you: **%%Plan:**
However, at the time of writing this wasn't working properly, and hadn't been working for quite some time. So if you do try this, don't be too surprised if it nobody can finger you.

ftp   To connect to an FTP site from Cix you just type ftp <site> See also the batchftp command which makes using Cix for ftp a lot friendlier.

gopher   To connect to the Cix Gopher system, just type gopher and then follow the instructions!

irc   Cix now has its own IRC client. IRC is Internet Relay Chat, as you should know if you have been reading the book properly! The Cix client attaches itself to a local IRC server, giving you a split screen with a small window at the bottom in which to type your message whilst watching everything else go whizzing by above. To use the IRC client it is advised that you set your terminal emulation to vt100.

ping   You can check to see if a site is alive by using Ping from the IP> prompt. Just enter ping <site>

quit   Exits the Internet subsystem and returns you to Cix at the main prompt.

receive	Allows you to upload a file into your Internet directory, ready for ftp to an Internet site.
rename	Renames any file stored in your Internet directory, useage is:

```
rename <oldname> <newname>
```

send	Download a file from your Internet directory to your computer.
strip	This is another of those really useful little commands that makes the Cix Internet Gateway such a joy to use. All it does is strip out all the odd characters out of filenames in your Internet directory, so as to prevent your computers operating system barfing on them. Characters such as <>{}[]\/"~&;`: will all get stripped out, as will any spaces.
telnet	To use the Cix telnet command to connect to remote site, just type telnet <site>
trace	This is another useful command that lets you see the connection route to any specified site. The more sites involved the slower the connection will be. To use just type: trace <site>
view	This command allows you to view a file, either binary or text. Bear in mind that both Cix and myself will tell you that viewing too many binary files like this will drive you crazy, OK! To use you just type VIEW <filename> This will place you into a pager with some nice features – here are the main commands:

=	Print more information about file
/	Start a forward search
?	Start a backwards search
b	Move back a page (24 lines)
f	Move forward a page (24 lines)
g	Move to top of file
G	Move to end of file
j	Move forward 1 line
k	Move back 1 line

n	Find next occurence of specified text
N	Move to next file in list to view
P	Move to previous file in list to view
q	Quit the pager, return to IP> prompt
r	Redraw screen

whois   Use whois to find out more information about a specified name. Just type:

`whois <name>`

www   To access the Cix World Wide Web client software you just type "www" at the IP> prompt. Cix doesn't, at the time of writing, provide a graphical WWW browser. The Cix client software is Lynx, which is a character based browser. Although you can't see the graphics whilst browsing, like you would with Mosaic for example, you can elect to download them to your machine to view later. This does have the advantage of speeding up your travels through the Web, but obviously isn't as attractive or appealing as using a graphical browser to fully exploit the power of World Wide Web.

Using Lynx is pretty simple. You can get online help from any point in your travels by using the "?" or "H" key. This will transport you to the site where

The Cix character based WWW browser.

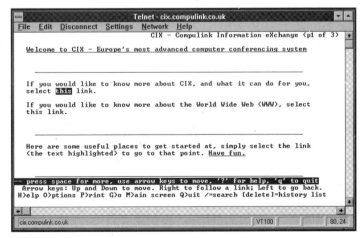

Lynx was developed, and give you access to the online user manual. Much of the navigation using Lynx can be accomplished using the numeric keypad, and the cursor keys as follows:

Keypad	Function
1	Move to end of text
3	Move down a page
7	Move to top of text
9	Move up a page
Cursor	Function
Up	Select previous link
Down	Select next link
Left	Back to previous document
Right	Display selected link

Cix has graphical WWW pages, but these are only accessible from outside of Cix. It's a funny old world sometimes!

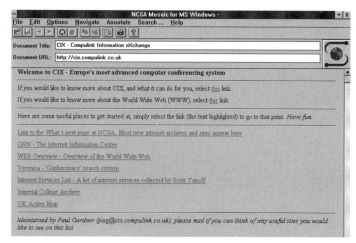

The following keyboard commands will also be helpful in your exploration of the Web using Lynx:

Keyboard	Key Function
Backspace	Show history list of current session
=	Shows information about current document
/	Activate search for a word within document
G	URL selector

I	Get an index of documents
M	Go to the starting document
O	Display Lynx options menu
P	Display print options menu
Z	Stop current process

USENET news on Cix

Cix offers two ways, essentially, of bringing you Usenet news. You can either use the online newsreader, which is based on the popular "trn" program, or you can do the whole thing offline by using an Off Line Reader such as Ameol. Let's take a look at the online method first.

To access the online newsreader, at the Main: or Read: prompts type:

GO NEWSNET

This will display a welcome message if this is your first time using the system, otherwise you will find yourself straight at the Newsnet prompt. To get to the interactive newsreader itself, you then need to type:

READER

Once started, the newsreader will present you with all newsgroups for which there is unread news and ask you if you want to read it or not. You can subscribe to newsgroups. Don't worry it doesn't cost anything, you just type:

g <newsgroup name>

To get a list of all available newsgroups you type:

1

When you have a newsgroup that you wish to read just press your enter key and you will find yourself magically placed into read mode. Make sure that threading has been enable as this makes things a lot easier to follow. To do

All you need to know about the Internet

this you need to enter the following command before you enter a newsgroup for reading:

You can now read your Usenet News, and post your own messages, reply to postings, etc etc. For full details of how to do this please refer to either the current Cix Manual or the online help available for the newsreader. It would fill half this book to actually go through all the avialable commands here!

USENET news offline

If you want the really easy way to participate in Usenet newsgroups, then get yourself a decent Off Line Reader. I use Ameol which is the "officially supported" Cix OLR, and it makes using Usenet extraordinarily simple. You can join and resign Usenet newsgroups at the click of a mouse button, and read and reply to postings as if they were just ordinary Cix conferences. And that is the beauty of using something like Ameol, it provides you with an apparently seamless interface to Usenet. I'd certainly recommend it to anyone who wants to get the best out of Usenet via Cix.

There are currently approaching 15,000 members of Cix, which has been expanding at a rapid rate during the past couple of years.

There are no surcharges for using Cix to access the Internet, but Cix is a time based service . Cix costs £25.00 to join, and then there are charges of £3.60 per hour peak rate (Mon – Fri, 8.00am – 5.00pm) and £2.40 at all other times, subject to a minimum monthly charge of £6.25

For more information about Cix, you should use the following contact methods:

Write to:
Compulink Information Exchange,
The Sanctuary,
Oakhill Grove,
Surbiton,
Surrey KT6 6DU

Phone 081 390 8446
Email **cixadmin@cix.compulink.co.uk**

Access with CompuServe

Although CompuServe is probably the biggest commercial on-line system, with more than 2.2 Million members world-wide and around 60,000 of those in the UK, its Internet access is severely lagging behind the other systems covered here. At the time of writing, CompuServe offers only Internet email and access to Usenet newsgroups, although Internet connectivity and provision is high on the list of development priorities for 1994/1995. Actually that isn't quite all as you can also Telnet into, but not out of, CompuServe.

Internet email

CompuServe was amongst the first of the on-line services to offer its members Internet email, providing the service way back in 1989.

It's easy enough to send email from CompuServe, although not as easy as Cix (who seem to have a monopoly on really friendly email facilities).

WinCIM makes CompuServe a really easy to use system, but Internet access is very limited at the time of writing.

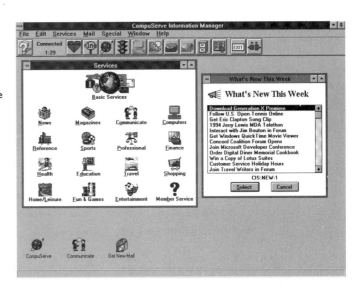

All you need to know about the Internet

Internet email needs to be addressed in a particular way, so if you were sending a message to me at my Delphi address you would need to type:

`INTERNET:waveydavey@delphi.com`

The main problem, as far as I am concerned, with the CompuServe when it comes to Internet mail is that they charge their users for receiving it. They also allow users the option of not accepting incoming mail from an external address if they don't want to pay for it, so you can get the scenario where you can't actually send email from the Internet to all CompuServe users.

Usenet news on CIS

CompuServe has recently introduced access to Usenet, and very nice it is to. Access to Usenet newsgroups is charged at the same rate as forums, that is at the Extended Service rate. Neither Cix nor Delphi UK currently charge any extra for their Internet services, so CompuServe are somewhat isolated in this respect.

There are two methods of getting to Usenet with CompuServe. You can use either the ASCII newsreader, or the CIM version complete with "go faster" stripes. The ASCII newsreader is straightforward to use, and ensures users of any platform can enjoy the benefits of Usenet access. However, the CIM version really is very nice indeed, offering some time saving and useful features. I've been using the WinCIM Newsreader and it makes reading and posting Usenet News extremely straightforward. CompuServe carries a complete set of Newsgroups, but only lists "selected" groups as available. This is because of the nature of some groups, which may offend a family audience, and also because there are just too many groups to list them all! All the other groups are available if you know their full name and you can subscribe to them directly. Otherwise you can subscribe to a newsgroup by browsing the available lists.

If you are using the CIM Newsreader you should bear in mind that all messages disappear after you have read them, so if any posting is of particular interest you should use the "hold" function to mark it as such.

The CompuServe WinCIM Newsreader is really rather spiffing.

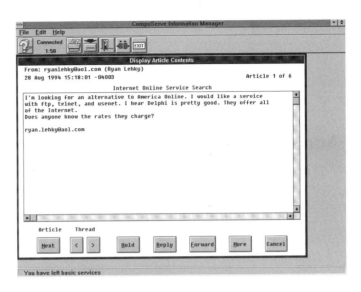

There are no Off Line Readers that can deal with Usenet access from CompuServe, to my knowledge, as I write. This situation is likely to change before too long, and this will reduce the cost of what is currently a fairly expensive way of getting your news!

If you know the subject you are interested in but not which newsgroups cover it, then use the "search" facility in the CIM Newsreader. For example, specifying "internet" will list all groups that contain that word in their name or description. You can then mark the check-box against all the groups you want to join and subscribe to them in one swoop.

CompuServe charges according to a time based system, on top of which many of its services carry a surcharge for use. For full details of pricing you should contact CompuServe at the address given below. CompuServe charges are in US Dollars, so you need to take the exchange rate into account when working out payments!

Write to
**CompuServe Information Service (UK),
1 Redcliff Street,
PO Box 676,**

All you need to know about the Internet

Bristol,
BS99 1YN

Phone **0800 289458**

Access with Delphi

Delphi Internet is one of the "big five" on-line systems in the United States, with over 100,000 members. Now Delphi has arrived in the UK, and provides a "Dial Up" connection to the Internet. The disadvantages of this type of connection have already been explored on the section about Cix. The advantages that using Delphi offers are, however, different to those presented by Cix, and are:

1) No hassle in setting up software, as it has all been done for your, regardless of your chosen computing platform.

2) Access to many Internet features are very simple indeed. Such things as Gophers, Telnet, and Usenet Newsgroups being just a menu choice away.

3) You get a value added service, as well as access to the Internet. Delphi UK gives full access to the American Delphi system as well, between the two

The Delphi UK Main menu.

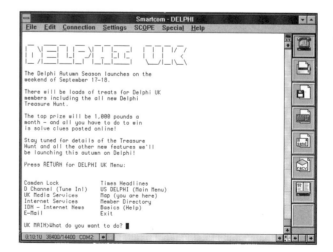

you have hundreds of discussion and support forums, Gigabytes of files on-line for you to download, shopping facilities, news headlines on-line from The Times, Sunday Times, Sky News and more, full email facilities, and even the chance to win £1000 in a monthly "Treasure Hunt" competition which is based in the "WaveyDavey" area where you can also join Delphi's own "On-line Jockey" (that's me folks) for some light-hearted chat and instant access to some interesting and weird Gophers and Usenet Newsgroups.

4) There is a well established Internet "SIG" (Special Interest Group) available to offer all the on-line advice you could want. The Host of this area, Walt Howe, has even written a book along with Steve Lambert which is all about accessing the Internet using Delphi!

The Delphi Internet SIG, well established and well useful.

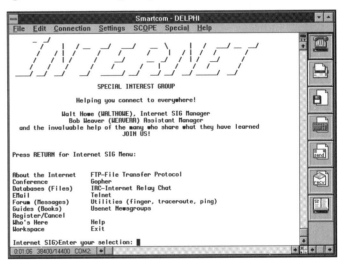

Internet Daily News

Typing IDN from the main Delphi UK prompt takes you to the Internet Daily News Area. Here you will find all sorts of publications offering news on and about the Internet, including the Daily Planet and Hotwired.

Internet email

Sending email across the Internet isn't as simple as it is with Cix, for example. You need to enter the Mail system, obviously, but it isn't then just a case of typing the full email address for the intended mail destination.

All you need to know about the Internet

Instead, you need to tell the Delphi Mail system that the email is intended to go out over the Internet, and you do this by typing the following at the To: prompt

`INTERNET"<email address>"`

So to send email to me as another Delphi user you would only have to specify my username at the To: prompt, like this:

`To: waveydavey`

But to send email to me over the Internet, say at my Demon Internet account, you would need to type:

`To: INTERNET"davey@wavey.demon.co.uk"`

Always make sure the email address is fully enclosed in quotes, that is both at the start and finish. Initially I forgot to use the final set of quotes and email would never get sent!

To save time, you don't have to type INTERNET at the To: prompt, you can shorten this to: IN%

Getting Started

Delphi has a number of utilities that make navigating the Internet as easy as possible – not surprising since Delphi US was amongst the first of the big on-line systems to offer its members Internet access some years ago. The easiest way to access parts of the Internet with Delphi is by using the menus that you will find in most of the SIGs or Areas.

Using my own Area as an example, within the WaveyDavey SIG you will find Usenet Newsgroups, Gopher and Telnet sites, both available from a simple menu structure. The "Wizard" of each Area on Delphi can set up these Internet Menus and just by selecting a menu number you will be automatically connected. A Delphi "Wizard" is the person who runs the area in question. For the Usenet side of things, selecting a newsgroup from the menu will place you straight into an interactive newsreader from where you can both read and reply to messages.

The Gopher Menus from the WaveyDavey area of Delphi.

The Gopher and Telnet menus allow you to connect straight to any specified Gopher, or Telnet site such as on-line games, as is the case from the WaveyDavey area. This is, without doubt, my favourite way of quickly accessing selected Internet resources. However, you will still want to be able to get to the exact resources you want rather than be limited to what a Delphi Wizard has chosen. Luckily you can do this and still use these simple menu structures, by building up your own "Personal Favourites" file. This will always be at the top of every Internet access menu you come across, and will always refer to your personal favourites and nobody else's. To build your file, you just use the normal Gopher, Telnet and Usenet menus and when you find something that is of interest just type:

SAVE

This item will now be added to your very own "Personal Favourites" menu, as a numbered menu item, and whenever you select that item you will be automatically connected straight to that resource!

All you need to know about the Internet

The Internet SIG

Most of Delphi's Internet access is done through the Internet SIG (Special Interest Group). From the main Delphi menu just type INTERNET, or from anywhere else type GO INTERNET, and you will be magically transported to the US Delphi system and into the Internet SIG at no extra cost your good self. Here you will be presented with options that cover every part of the Internet, including lots of help in actually finding your way around.

Much like the "internet" conference on Cix, here you will find lots of files to download which contain Internet tools, utilities, documentation and so on, as well as forums where Internet experts will be happy to help you out with your questions and problems.

○ **Typing FTP** at the Internet SIG> prompt, will allow you to enter a ftp sitename and connect easily if you just follow the prompts.

○ **Typing GOPHER** at the Internet SIG> prompt brings up the Internet SIG Gopher, which is your gateway to all sorts of helpful and useful resources. This is also your gateway to the WWW with Delphi, but is only a character based system due to the nature of the Internet connection as explained before.

○ **Typing IRC** places you in Internet Relay Chat mode, and gives some useful on-line help about using the system as well. Typing TELNET allows you to specify sites to telnet to, unsurprisingly enough, and Email takes you to the mail prompt.

○ **Typing UTILITIES** is very interesting, and takes you to a menu where you can select from such useful tools as Finger, Netfind, Ping, and Traceroute.

Usenet news on Delphi

Participating on Usenet is just so easy on Delphi, either by using the Usenet menus available from most Areas or by using the Usenet option from the Internet SIG> prompt.

Once you type USENET from the Internet SIG> prompt you are presented with a number of options. Typing USENET again will take you into the

**The Utilities menu
at DelphiUK.**

Delphi Usenet Newsreader, which presents you with a large menu of options.

As always, the first item is your own "Personal Favourites" menu, and then you can choose from text giving you help on various aspects of using Usenet and using the reader, as well as various ways of actually connecting directly to the Usenet Newsgroup of your choice. It's all very, very simple to use and designed in such a way that it soon becomes second nature.

Delphi charges are time based, but they offer a choice of two pricing plans. The first is called the 10/4 plan. This costs £10.00 per month, for which the first four hours use each month is included, and after that each hour costs £4.00 until the end of that month.

The second is the 20/20 Plan, which costs £20.00 per month, giving 20 hours use, after which each hour will cost you just £1.80 until the end of the month. Delphi also run an introductory offer to the system which lets you have 5 hours free use to look around before you decide if you want to subscribe or not!

For more information about Delphi contact them thus:

Reading the Usenet News, Delphi style.

Write to
Delphi Internet UK,
The Elephant House,
Hawley Crescent,
London,
NW1 8NP

Email **uk@delphi.com**
Phone **071 757 7080**

Access with the PC User Group

The PC User Group has been offering Internet services for more than six years now, and provides two main, and quite distinct, services. The first is the Interactive Premium Service, which gives you access to the CONNECT bulletin board system, and from there such things as interactive ftp, character based World Wide Web access, gopher, telnet, archie, and irc as well as email, conferencing, games, and online file areas. You access the CONNECT BBS using your favourite comms software. Usenet News and Internet Email are normally accessed via the second of the PC User Group services, and that is WinNET.

WinNET is a Windows interface that makes reading and positng email and Usenet News both simple and cheap. Simple because, for a novice user, the WinNET program is a delight to use with everything being very intuitive and well designed. The program is incredibly easy to install and setup, you only need to spend a couple of minutes answering questions about your PC and software, select an email address, and it is ready to use. Cheap because WinNET is an offline reader for email and Usenet!

WinNET in all its simple glory.

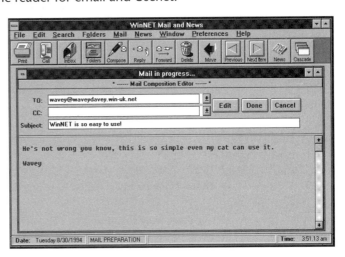

I've been using this program for some time now, and while it isn't as powerful as many of the other email programs available (no support for MIME as an example) it does have the advantage of the offline support for Usenet in a Windows environment. In fact there are a number of nice touches, not least the "scheduler" program that allows you to set up a regular daily connect schedule, and get WinNET to go and collect your awaiting email and Usenet News for you without you having to be there to do it! WinNET was devloped by the wonderfully named "Computer Witchcraft Inc" from Louisville in the USA, and I mention this fact for no other reason than I really like the name of that company.

The PC User Group would seem ideally suited for those of you who would like email and Usenet access but are not sure about wanting, or needing, a full Internet service just yet. The WinNET program is wonderful for this, as it allows such things as archie and ftp by email using the Mail Servers at the

All you need to know about the Internet

Usenet support
from WinNET.

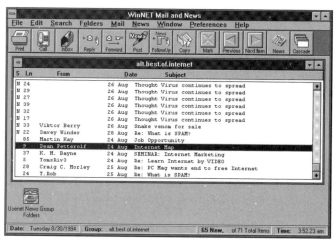

PC User group HQ. Local access is available via points of Presence in Birmingham, Bristol, Cambridge, Edinburgh, and Manchester as well as the London host, and more are planned. And, of course, if you get hooked and find you need fuller access to Internet services you can always extend your membership to include the Premium Services as mentioned.

MAKE A
NOTE!

There are currently in the region of 10,000 subscribers to the PC User Group, who also offer computer equipment insurance at reasonable rates, and produce a monthly magazine for its members.

So how much does all this cost? Not that much, is the somewhat surprising answer! WinNET software comes free of charge on a one disk package direct from the PC User Group. To setup an account will cost £6.75 per month, which includes 130 minutes of connect time, with subsequent connect time being charged at £3.25 an hour. It is worth remembering though that because this is an off-line system you are unlikely to exceed the 130 minutes of connect time each month (a typical daily connection takes less than 3 mintues).

If you want the Interactive Premium Service, then that costs a further £7.25 per month, but there are no time charges to apply to this account.

For more information about the PC User Group, you should use the following contact methods:

Write to
PC User Group,
PO Box 360,
84-88 Pinner Road,
Harrow
HA1 4LQ

Phone **081 863 1191**
Email **help@win-uk.net or info@ibmpcug.co.uk**

Using the dial-in dedicated providers

What do you mean by 'dedicated providers?' I hear you ask. I also hear me answering, "The ones that provide a dial-in SLIP/PPP direct connection to the Internet."

The advantages of this type of connection were explained in some detail towards the start of the book, but in case you read books like my young lady and skip to the back first, here's a review.

WHAT
DOES IT
MEAN

Dial-In providers offer a full connection, giving access to graphical World Wide Web browsers such as Mosaic, as well as the possibility of your own personal domain on the Internet (for example, using Demon I am davey@wavey.demon.co.uk but using the services of the PC User Group I become wavey@waveydavey.win-uk.net).

You also tend to pay only a monthly, or yearly, membership fee with unlimited on-line time at no extra charge, however I'd recommend checking this out with your provider rather than taking it for granted!

This type of service provider is fast becoming one of the growth industries of the 90s, there seem to be new ones popping up all over the place. This may be a blessing or a curse, depending on your viewpoint. Certainly there is room in the marketplace for a number of quality services, but that number is surely limited. The danger is that some of the companies that are appearing will be disappearing almost as quickly, once the market settles itself out. And remember that many such services are asking for a year's worth of membership fees in advance. Wavey's advice is take a careful look at the company concerned before shelling out your hard-earned wad!

In this section I am concentrating on just a few of the many service providers that could fall into this category. The ones I am looking at have either been around for a long time (in the Internet plan of things that is) or have the backing of a major player in the marketplace. They are also companies of whom I have personal experience – have actually used – and so can pass back my own experiences and impressions of the service. Once again, I am making no recommendations here, that isn't my job, I am merely giving you the ammunition you need to be able to load up your thinking gun and fire off a decision.

Access with the BBC Networking Club

The BBC may at first seem an unusual concern to want to get in on the Internet provision act. But if you think about it, it makes perfect sense. The "Information Superhighway" opens up all sorts of possibilities for electronic publishing and broadcasting, and why should the BBC not be involved? After all, 1994 has seen two BBC programmes about computing and comms, "The Big Byte" on Radio 5, and "The Net" on BBC 2 (where you may have even seen Wavey Davey on the very first episode).

The BBC Networking Club, hereafter referred to by its acronym of BBCNC, was launched during the Summer of 1994 and started to build up a healthy membership right away. Their service includes a dedicated BBC Bulletin Board called "Auntie" as well as access to all the usual Internet facilities using, for the most part, public domain and shareware applications that have been setup to be BBCNC friendly where possible.

The **BBCNC**
WWW Pages
are very well
put together

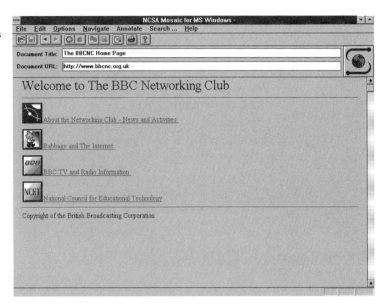

Technical and user support comes in the form of a "buddy" system, where experienced users help out those who are just joining the fold. The BBCNC is restricted to over 16s only, and even allowing for this they have decided to only make certain Usenet Newsgroups available. This isn't to say you don't get a lot of choice, but you won't find the more "adult" groups here. However, for me, the biggest single drawback to this system is the fact that at present you can only use the email facilities through the Auntie BBS, which means you can't use your favourite Mail program and have to compose and read messages online.

The BBCNC also has its own World Wide Web pages which are becoming really quite impressive, offering the chance to participate in programme feedback as well as giving listings of TV and Radio broadcasts.

The BBCNC costs £25 initially, and then £12 per month to use. This includes the price of software to PC, Mac, and Acorn users (Acorn users must pay £35 as the initial fee for some reason). If you use an Amiga or some other computer platform then I'm afraid you are not catered for in the software department!

For more information about the BBC Networking Club, you should use the following contact methods:

Write to
BBC Networking Club,
PO Box 7,
Broadcasting Support Services,
London W3 6XY

Phone **081 576 7799**
Email **info@bbcnc.org.uk**

Access with CityScape

CityScape, in collaboration with PIPEX, are aiming at making Internet access as easy as possible with its IP.GOLD service for users of Microsoft Windows. IP.GOLD incorporates three programs in its package, which comes with a very easy to use install program. You just put the supplied floppy into the drive, type setup, and that's it. This really is a one stop Internet provision solution.

The Global On-Line pages at CityScape's Web HQ.

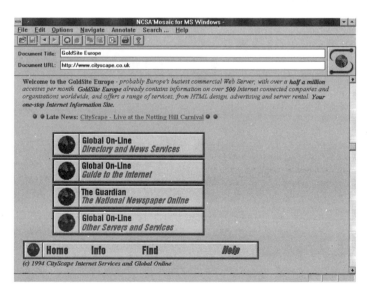

The software suite comprises three parts – a mail program, Usenet newsreader, and a World Wide Web browser. The newsreader is a public domain one, and the World Wide Web browser is a customised version of Mosaic (customised to include menu entries for the CityScape WWW pages that is). The mail program is the only actual commercial part of the package, and takes the form of Mail-It 2.0 from Unipalm.

Mail-It is a very nice program, fully functional with MIME support, which is a native Windows application so should be quite familiar and easy to use even if you don't know your email from your elbow. Mail-It can be configured to automatically check for new email, has a nice address book, and even supports international languages.

Using Mosaic you can connect to the CityScape WWW pages which are very well put together, and provide a wealth of information not only about CityScape itself but also cyberspace in general.

The CityScape World Wide Web home page could be your gateway to the Internet.

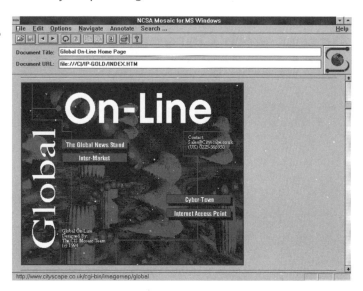

All this ease of use and "out of the box" functionality doesn't come cheap, and CityScape are currently one of the more expensive of the dedicated service providers. The initial setting up fee is £50, and that is followed by a yearly membership cost of £180. However, for your money you get unlimited technical support from the on-line help desk, a national network of POPs (Points Of Presence – making connection usually only a local phone call away) which have on-site engineers to help ensure 24 hour availability, and a guarantee of minimum user to modem ratios (but no mention of what these ratios are).

For more information about CityScape, you should use the following contact methods:

Write to
CityScape Internet Services Ltd,
59 Wycliffe Road,
Cambridge CB1 3JE

Phone **0223 566950**
Email **sales@cityscape.co.uk**

Access with Demon

Demon Internet Limited have been, to a large degree, pioneers in the area of Internet service provision in the UK. Or to be more precise, pioneers in the area of affordable Internet servcie provision. Demon Internet was born out of the notion that if enough people could be convinced to pledge subscriptions, then full Internet access could be available for only £10 per month (in fact the conference on Cix that was created to establish interest, and still survives as a support forum, was called **tenner.a.month**). Enough people were convinced and, after many months of planning and hard work, Demon came to life in June 1992.

Although the original idea was that Demon would be able to offer this low cost approach because its customers would be technically capable and therefore require little in the way of support, this has now changed. Demon have grown to become one of the leading players in the UK marketplace with approaching 10,000 members as I write, and as such cater for the needs of all levels of customer. They have telephone support lines which are

available until 9pm on weekdays, and 5pm weekends and employ 6 support
staff.

**The Demon "DIS"
interface is simple
but effective**

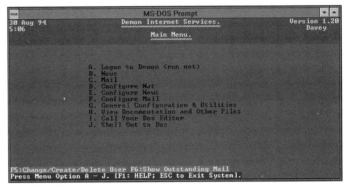

Another feature of the Demon service is the availability of POPs, points of
presence, that allow the user to be able to use the system by making a local
phone call. Currently there are more than 270 telephone lines covering
areas including, London, Birmingham, Cambridge, Edinburgh, Reading,
Sunderland, Warrington, and Yorkshire. New POPs are always being
developed to bring the service closer to more and more people.

**Demons Points of
Presence, as
shown on the
Demon WWW
Pages.**

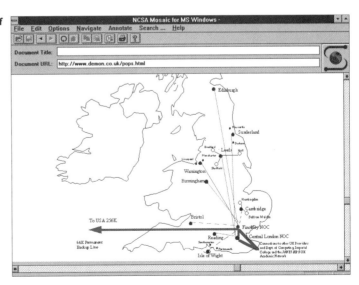

Joining Demon is fairly easy, although there is an assumption that you already have some comms knowledge and software. When you join you receive instructions on how to download the software that is required for your particular platform from the Demon download account. This account has a password which changes daily, so you have to telephone the Demon office to get the correct password for the day you want to retrieve the software. Once you connect to this account, using your standard communications package (which it is assumed you already have) you just follow the on-screen prompts to collect the appropriate Demon software required. For the purposes of the examples used here I am assuming you will be using the standard DOS-based package.

The software comes in a self extracting archive, will extract to its own subdirectory and unpack its contents. These include readme files which you should consult as to how to proceed. Once the software is setup and ready to use, you need to find out your Internet address and choose a password, then you connect to Demon using a standard comms package and enter your host name, that's the name of your machine at Demon not your username, at the login prompt (so mine would be `wavey.demon.co.uk`). This will take you into a password selection program, after which you will be given your Internet address in numerical format (an IP number). Make sure you remember your password and note down the IP number, you won't be able to use your account if you don't have these!

As well as access to all Internet applications and services, Demon has a few of it's own. There is an excellent FTP site at Demon, where you can get all the latest programs to make Internet life easier. The Demon World Wide Web pages are developing into a very useful information resource, and Demon has a number of its own, local, Usenet newsgroups for support and information purposes.

Much of the routine Internet access for many users can be carried out off-line using the supplied Demon software. Basically email can be composed and read off-line, as can Usenet news. The software is fully functional and pretty easy to use if you read the documentation!

Take Wavey's advice. If you are using Demon for the first time and want to subscribe to Usenet Newsgroups, prevent yourself from being logged in forever and collecting literally thousands of messages by changing the "date you last got news" option in your DIS software by doing the following BEFORE you connect for the first time:

From the DIS Main Menu select option E - Configure News. Then select option C - Maintain Date You Last Got News. You can select from the following options by pressing the required Function key, the fewer days the less News you will get, the more days the more News and the longer it will take and the more disk space you will sacrifice!

F4 = I day
F5 = 2 days
F6 = 3 days
F7 = 4 days
F8 = 5 days
F9 = 6 days
FI0 = I week
After you have made your choice, select F3 to update the software.

Limiting the date from which you first collect your Usenet news is important if you want to avoid a costly and time consuming exercise.

```
                               MS-DOS Prompt                    ▼ ▲
30 Aug 94            Demon Internet Services.              Version 1.20
5:12                                                            Davey
               Maintain the Date You Last Got News.

       Date You Last Last Successfully
       Received a Complete set of News  29 Aug 1994

                            Time  20:55   (the seconds will set to 0)
                                          This is GMT

       This alters the time and date in a file called NNTP.DAT.  You
       should never need to alter this file by hand although you may
       do so through the Advanced Editing submenu.


 Note the Function Keys take days from *today's* date.

 F4:1 Day Ago   F5:2 Days   F6:3 Days   F7:4 Days   F8:5 Days   F9:6 Days   F10:1 Week
 Enter the Time [F1:Help; ESC:Abort; F3:Update].
```

Demon offer many different service options, the standard dial-up account costs £12.50 registration fee and then £10.00 per month after that, there are no on-line time charges. There are also a number of options to suit the corporate user including network connections, reserved lines, and 64K leased lines.

For more information about Demon, you should use the following contact methods:

Write to
Demon Internet Limited,
42 Hendon Lane,
Finchley,
London N3 1TT

Phone **081 349 0063** or **031 552 0344**
Email `internet@demon.net`

Access with The Direct Connection

The Direct Connection might not be a name that you recognise, but they have been involved in on-line communications since 1986. They offer two main services of interest here, the first being a direct connection to the Internet by means of a TCP/IP account, the second being their own on-line system which has pretty good Internet provision of its own.

The TCP/IP account supports either SLIP or PPP connections, and is a straightforward Internet connection providing all that the Internet has to offer. The Direct Connection doesn't provide any software, that choice is left to up to you, but I've been using Chameleon with no problems whatsoever. Technical support is very good, and I've not found there to be any problem in actually getting through so the modem to user ratios must be quite high.

The Login accounts give access to The Direct Connection on-line service, and this offers a pretty good "Dial-Up" Internet connection (text based World Wide The Direct Connection on-line serviceWeb, access to ftp, gophers, archie etc) as well as Usenet News, Fax facilities, Email, File areas, and "Computer Newswire" which offers Newsbytes and Associated Press news headlines.

The Direct Connection on-line service.

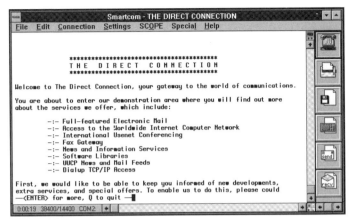

```
─                    Smartcom - THE DIRECT CONNECTION              ▼ ▲
 File  Edit  Connection  Settings  SCOPE  Special  Help

                 *******************************************
                 T H E   D I R E C T   C O N N E C T I O N
                 *******************************************
         Welcome to The Direct Connection, your gateway to the world of communications.

         You are about to enter our demonstration area where you will find out more
         about the services we offer, which include:

                    -:- Full-featured Electronic Mail
                    -:- Access to the Worldwide Internet Computer Network
                    -:- International Usenet Conferencing
                    -:- Fax Gateway
                    -:- News and Information Services
                    -:- Software Libraries
                    -:- UUCP News and Mail Feeds
                    -:- Dialup TCP/IP Access

         First, we would like to be able to keep you informed of new developments,
         extra services, and special offers. To enable us to do this, please could
         —<ENTER> for more, Q to quit —▊
 0:00:19 38400/14400 COM2  ◆
```

The costs vary according to what type of account you want, but all accounts carry a once only registration fee of £7.50

Standard Login account is £10.00 per month (Email, Usenet, BBS services)

Enhanced Login account is £20.00 per month (As above plus Dial-Up Internet access)

TCP/IP account is £10.00 per month (Full direct Internet connection, no BBS access)

All these prices are for unlimited access, there are no additonal time based charges.

For more information about The Direct Connection, you should use the following contact methods:

Write to
The Direct Connection,
 PO Box 931,
London,
SE18 3PW

Phone **081 317 0100**
Email **helpdesk@tdc.dircon.co.uk**

All you need to know about the Internet

Chapter 23

Cyber-Societies

There are a number of organisations involved in ensuring the continued development of the Internet, protecting the people who use it, and promoting public awareness of computer based communications. Of these, the following deserve special mention, and I would certainly recommend that you take a closer look at each organisation, even if you don't get an uncontrollable urge to join up!

Care in the CommUnity, the UK perspective

CommUnity is the Computer Communicators' Association, and came into being in the final few weeks of 1992. There had been a threat to the survival of Bulletin Board Systems from the combined forces of FAST (the Federation Against Software Theft) and ELSPA (the European Leisure Software Publishers Association). In an effort to try and reduce software theft and piracy, which these organisations perceived was rife on BBS's, they were looking at the possibility of getting legislation to enforce the licensing of Bulletin Boards and On-Line Systems.

The on-line community soon got to hear about these plans, helped along the way by an article I wrote on the very subject for Amiga Shopper magazine, and decided that they needed a concerted effort to ensure that such legislation should not be allowed to threaten the very existence of BBSs (many of which are run on small budgets, without charging their members, and who would have to close if forced to pay a hefty license fee every year). The result of this was a meeting in London where representatives of all the main networks were present. A committee was elected to investigate what could be done, and how to do it, and I was proud to be elected to serve as part of the steering group. It was from these seeds that CommUnity, The Computer Communicators' Association was born. Fortunately, the proposed legislation got nowhere, and following a meeting with FAST, ELSPA, an MP, and members of the on-line community the plans were dropped.

CommUnity however has continued to grow from strength to strength, and is the UK's leading organisation of and for users of on-line systems and networks. With a regular electronic journal called "CommUnicator" and a

CommUnicator is
the journal of
CommUnity, and
is distributed
across the
Internet, of course

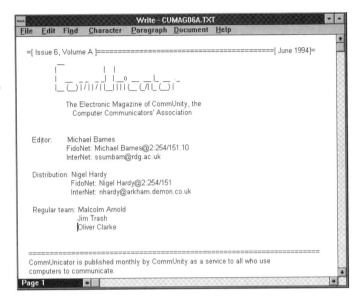

presence on many BBSs as well as the Internet, I am certain that it will continue so to do.

The aims of the Computer Communicators' Association are:

1) To maintain and connect a membership which shares a common concern that access to technology, information, and communication should be as freely available as possible.

2) To raise public awareness about issues and opportunities arising from ongoing rapid advances in computer-based communications media.

3) To monitor and inform the press and media of computer-based communications, responding to misinformation or prejudice with a coherent voice.

4) To develop among policy makers a better understanding of the issues underlying free and open telecommunications, and support legal and structural approaches which ease the assimilation of new technologies by society, and maintain open access to them.

All you need to know about the Internet

5) To support litigation in the public interest to preserve, protect, and extend civil rights within the realm of computing and telecommunications technology.

6) To work with agencies and individuals who share our interest in the development of computer-based communications.

7) To extend our membership and organisation to include wider Europe, or assist there in the establishment and networking of independent groups sharing our aims.

8) To encourage and support educational activities and initiatives which increase popular understanding of the opportunites and challenges posed by developments in computing and telecommunications.

9) To encourage and support the development of new tools which ease access to computer-based telecommunications.

The CommUnity constitution also leaves us in no doubt as to what the Computer Communicators' Association isn't, stating that they:

"...shall not seek to control or enforce specific conduct in computer communications users, on-line systems or networks. Shall not enter into any relationship with any other group wherein it becomes required, encouraged or obliged to actively monitor on-line systems, networks or activities for any person. Shall not act as intermediary between complainants or informants and other groups or agencies for the purpose of passing on allegations of, information on, or evidence of activities by computer communications users, online services or networks."

To find out more about CommUnity you can send email to `community@arkham.demon.co.uk` or join the Usenet Newsgroup `uk.org.community`

Files relating to CommUnity are available by FTP from:

`ftp.demon.co.uk/pub/archives/community`

The Computer Communicators' Association was originally set up as a voluntary organisation, but funds are always needed to cover the basic administrative costs and to help with lobbying. So to do your bit in ensuring that your rights as an on-line user are protected, why not join CommUnity by sending a cheque for £10.00 (£5.00 if unemployed or a student) made payable to "CommUnity" to the following address:

CommUnity
89 Mayfair Avenue
Worcester Park
Surrey KT4 7SJ

Enclose a short signed letter requesting membership which must include the following details:

Full name, postal address, email address, and any other information you think may be useful along with your permission to store these details in the CommUnity membership database.

Kings of the Wild Frontier – USA perspective

The EFF, Electronic Frontier Foundation, is a longer established but similar organisation to the Computer Communicators' Association here in the UK. The EFF was born out of a conviction amongst its founders that an organisation was required to address the democratic potential of new computer communications technology. Founded way back (hey, it's a heck of a long time in Cyberspace) in 1990, the Electronic Frontier Foundation has the following mission statement:

"Our primary mission is to ensure that the new electronic highways emerging from the convergence of telephone, cable, broadcast, and other communications technologies enhance First and Fourth Amendment rights, encourage new entrepreneurial activity, and are open and accessible to all segments of society.

The EFF,
frontiersmen of
the new age.

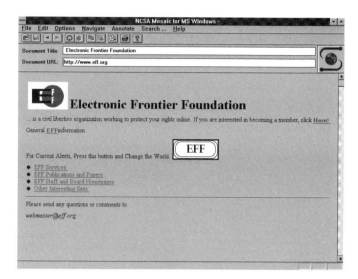

While well established legal principles and cultural norms give structure and coherence to uses of convential media like newspapers, books, and telephones, the new digital media do not easily fit into existing frameworks. Conflicts come about as the law struggles to define its application in a context where fundamental notions of speech, property, and place take profoundly news forms. People sense both the promise and the threat inherent in new computer and communications technologies, even as they struggle to master or simply cope with them in the work place and the home. The technologies and market structures that enhance communications and the flow of information may also pose serious threats to personal privacy.

The Electronic Frontier Foundation is committed to ensuring that the rules, regulations, and laws being applied to emerging communications technologies are in keeping with our society's highest traditions of the free and open flow of ideas and information whilse protecting personal privacy."

To find out more about the EFF, who produce (shock horror) actual printed on paper booklets as well as electronic versions, send email to
eff@eff.org

Files pertaining to the Electronic Frontier Foundation are available by FTP from:

`ftp.eff.org`

There is also an EFF Mailing List and a Usenet Newsgroup, respectively:

`eff-request@eff.org and comp.org.eff.news`

Supporting Cyberspace, The Internet Society

The Internet Society is the parent body to the Internet Architecture Board, an important group whose role is with technical and policy issues regarding the evolution of the architecture of the Internet. An international body, The Internet Society doesn't run the Internet (nobody runs the Internet, everyone just borrows a bit of it) but it does work to keep it well oiled and running smoothly. The Internet Society charter has the following goals:

1) To facilitate and support the technical evolution of the Internet as a research and eductaion infrastructure, and to stimulate the involvement of the scientific community, industry, government and others in the evolution of the Internet.

2) To educate the scientific community, industry and the public at large concerning the technology, use and application of the Internet.

3) To promot educational applications of Internet technology for the benefit of government, colleges and universities, industry and the public at large.

4) To provide a forum for exploration of new Internet applications, and to stimulate collaboration among organisations in their operational use of the global Internet.

**The Internet
Society WWW
pages.**

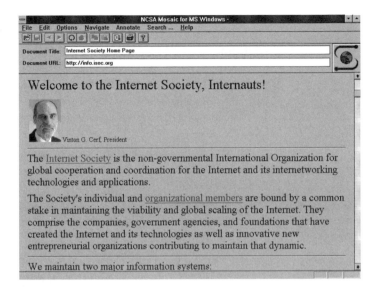

For more information about The Internet Society you can send email to
isoc@isoc.org

Chapter 24

FAQs

What is a FAQ? Well that was, actually.

FAQ stands for a Frequently Asked Question. You will find FAQs dotted all over the Internet, and very useful they are too. They will help you get the most out of whatever part of the Internet they refer to. It is a pretty good bet that the questions most people ask relate to the problems that crop up most often, and so you well face some of these. I've put together a FAQ file just for you, to help you deal with the most common questions that might crop up during your journey into cyberspace, so without further ado here it is:

Wavey Davey's Internet FAQ file

Q What's in an email header, it looks like a load of garbage to me?

A Well it's far from a load of garbage, for without much of that information the email would never arrive in your mailbox. Some, indeed rather a lot, of the information in a header details the route that the email has travelled in order to reach you. Not particularly interesting, but damn useful if email can't get where you want to send it. You can use this information to try and find out why your email is bouncing. The easiest way to think of an email header is like an ordinary envelope that a letter arrives in, sometimes it arrives with stuff the Post Office or Postman have written on it, especially if there have been problems finding your address.

Q I've managed to successfully, or so I thought, FTP a file from an anonymous FTP site to my computer. But when I try to unzip it, or if it is already unzipped try to run it, nothing happens. So what am I doing wrong?

A Before you FTP a file other than a simple text file, you need to make sure the transfer will be in binary mode. Many FTP sites default automatically to ASCII mode. Just type "binary" before you start to get the file and all will be OK.

Q Everybody seems to be talking about them, but what the heck is a URL?

A URLs are Unifrom Resource Locators, an attempt at standardising the format of Internet resource location addresses. A URL consists of a simple (once you know how they work) one line pathway to a resource. An example would be if I was trying to locate a file called "netiquette.txt" which is located in the internet.literature directory at `ftp.sura.net`, which is a mouthful yet still doesn't give you the full path needed, this would translate to a URL of:
`ftp://ftp.sura.net/pub/nic/internet.literature/¬`
`netiquette.txt`
The part before the colon indicates the access type, everything after the colon are the specific instructions. Generally speaking, the two slashes // after the colon indicate a site name.

Q What is an RFC?

A An RFC, or Request For Comments, is a working document that relates to the development of a standard, specification, or some other communications and Internet related item. RFC's are generally pretty boring things, unless you are a total propellor head, but are important as they help to shape the future of the Internet.

Q Can I advertise my services on the Internet?

A Hey Wavey, let's get into a really contentious area shall we? Well, although many Internet afficionados will tell you no, no way, absolutely not, never, THIS Internet afficionado will tell you the Internet is used for advertising, has always been used for advertising, and will continue to be used for advertising. The increasing commercialisation of the Internet will, of course, lead to more growth in the potential for business advertising. The thing to remember is to always follow existing and established etiquette, don't just Junk-Mail users or you will do more harm than good to your reputation. Internet advertising if researched well, and targeted efficiently, can be a very successful means of selling your wares.

All you need to know about the Internet **.net**

Q What is UNIX?

A UNIX is a massively popular, and indeed massive, operating system. It is available for a variety of computing platforms, and is a multi-user and maulti-tasking environment. For historical reasons you will find UNIX is the most prevalent operating system used on the Internet. Learning UNIX is a mammoth task, indeed there are many books devoted to this very subject. However, do not fear as I have provided all the basic command information you'll need to get your head around it in this very tome!

Q Can I be completely anonymous on the Internet?

A Not completely, no. However, there are ways for you to be able to send email and postings to Usenet Newsgroups in anonymity. The most popular, and by far the easiest, method is to use the services of an Anonymous Mail Server such as the one at **anon.penet.fi**

Just send email to **help@anon.penet.fi** for details of how to use this free service. Be warned though, that abuse of such a service (for example sending abusive or obscene postings via an Anonymous Mail Server) will only lead to the service being shut down.

Q How many Usenet Newsgroups are there?

A Some would say too many! Actually the latest figures I have, for the start of 1994, show that there are more than 7,000 groups. Expect that figure to have grown somewhat by the time you get to read this.

Q Is there really loads of pornographic material available from the Internet, if so how do I get it?

A There is SOME pornographic material on the Internet, mainly distributed via Usenet Newsgroups. Whether it is available or not depends on the Service Provider you use and if they give access to these newsgroups, some don't. The majority of dirty pictures are of pretty poor quality, the file sizes are large, they come as UUencoded messages which means that

you have to UUdecode tham after downloading, and are generally no
more explicit than the pictures contained in any top shelf magazine.
What I'm saying is that it is a pretty inefficient means of getting your
hands on some mucky pics. Ignore the hype and carry on buying
"Beautiful Babes" or whatever from the newsagent, if you really have to.

Q Are Signature Files really the spawn of Satan?

A No, but I can't blame you for thinking they might be, given the hostility
they receive from some Internet (and specifically Usenet) users. A sig file
can be as simple as just your initials or first name, and nobody has a
problem with that. What people do, for some strange reason, find
annoying is the really long signature. The one that is longer than the
message it is attached to, the one that is a blatant advertisement for a
service, the one that is designed to offend. A sig file of a few lines is fine,
make it too big and you better be wearing asbestos Y-fronts.

Q What's a Flame War?

A A Flame War is when two or more people start insulting and abusing
each other and just can't find it in themselves to stop. This course of
events comes about when you get a clash of egos, personalities, etc. Also
Flame Wars happen as a result of people disliking sig files, a particular
posting, oh for any reason really. It's like a couple of kids fighting in a
cake shop, very easy to start and a lot harder to stop, but a heck of a lot
of fun :-)

Q Can I send a FAX using the Internet?

A Well yes, you can, but you will need to be a member of an Internet
connected service that offers such a facility (like Cix or CompuServe for
example). But I guess that isn't really what you meant, is it? There is a
free fax service in the USA which is devloping right now, and if you send
some eEmail to **tpc-faq@town.hall.org** they will send you their FAQ
file about the service.

Q Are there any teapots on the Internet?

A Well there is Wavey Davey, who is totally teapot himself. There is, actually, a coffee pot on the Internet though. If you have a World Wide Web browser and point it in the direction of `http://www.cl.cam.ac.uk/coffee/coffee.html` you will find a realtime image of a coffee pot (updated every second in fact).

Q I have seen a few organisations who sell their services via the Internet, and they want me to purchase using my credit card. Is it safe to send these details over the Internet?

A Hmm, tricky question to answer. Personally I wouldn't send MY credit card details in this way purely because it is possible, although pretty unlikely, that someone could intercept and use the information. If you do send such details, make sure you email them in encrypted form using something like the Pretty Good Privacy (PGP) program.

Q What is Internet Talk Radio?

A Basically a very clever idea, but a none too practical reality for the home user. Internet Talk Radio is a 60 minute radio show that is distributed by FTP over the Internet. You get an audio file of the show to play back via your computer. One problem is that each show may consume about 30Mb of your hard disk space! Another problem is that I certainly am not that interested in going to all that trouble just to get an hour of conversation of the duffle coat and bottle bottom glasses variety!

Chapter 25

Smiley Dictionary

One of the problems faced by people both writing and reading email of any kind, be it a private email message or a public Usenet posting, is the ability to adequately express and, indeed, interpret emotion. Over the years a cunningly simple method of indicating emotional expression within text based messaging has developed, and is now in common use by millions of people every single day.

Smileys, or emote-icons as some of the sadder anorak wearing brigade like to call them, are a very quick, easy, and above all efficient means of aiding communication.

A sentence such as "Oh yes, and you would know all about it" could be interpreted in many different ways. The addition of a winking smiley would indicate it was meant jokingly, a plain smiley might mean it wasn't meant nastily, an evil smiley might mean you were just stirring things up, while no smiley whatsoever would indicate you bloody well meant it!

Of course smileys are not perfect, nothing is going to be able to compete with a face to face conversation for expressing emotion. Mistakes in interpretation are still made, but at least they are fewer than they would be without these loveable little creatures.

To view a smiley, turn the page sideways. You will now see that it represents a facial expression and start to understand the way that smileys work.

In this brief dictionary, I cannot hope to cover all the smiley variations that exist. Indeed, I wouldn't want to as some of them are really quite racist, sexist, disgusting, or just plain useless. I have, however, tried to provide you with enough weaponry to be able to go forth and conquer cyberspace!

Wavey Davey's Happy Haircut Smiley Dictionary

Smiley meaning

Smiley	meaning
:-||	Angry
(:-)	Bald
:-)	Basic happy
:-(	Basic sad
B-)	Batman
:-)>	Bearded
%+(	Beaten up
?-)	Black eye
:-)X	Bow tie
R-)	Broken glasses
:^)	Broken nose
|:-)	Bushy eyebrows
)	Cheshire cat
<|-)	Chinese
3:-)	Cow
:-t	Cross
X-)	Cross eyed
:'-(	Crying
i-)	Detective (private eye)
:-e	Disappointed
:-)'	Drooling
{:V	Duck
<:-)	Dumb question
5:-)	Elvis
>:-)	Evil grin
:'''-(	Floods of tears
:-!	Foot in mouth
/:-)	French
8)	Frog
::-)	Glasses wearer (1)
8-)	Glasses wearer (2)
8:)	Gorilla
:-')	Has a cold (1)

All you need to know about the Internet

:*)	Has a cold (2)
:-|	Hmmmph!
:-C	Jaw hits floor
.-)	Keeping an eye out
:-#	Kiss (1)
:-*	Kiss (2)
:-X	Kiss (3)
:+)	Large nose
:-D	Laughing out loud
:-}	Leering
(-:	Left handed
:-9	Licking lips
:-}	Lipstick wearer
:- |	Monkey
:-{	Moustache (1)
:-#)	Moustache (2)
(-)	Needs haircut
:^)	Nose out of joint
:8)	Pig
:-?	Pipe smoker
=:-)	Punk
:-"	Pursed lips
|-]	Robocop
O:-)	Saint
:-@	Screaming
:-O	Shocked
:-V	Shouting
|-)	Sleeping
:-i	Smoker (1)
:-Q	Smoker (2)
:-j	Smoker smiling
:-6	Sour taste in mouth
:-v	Speaking
:-w	Speaks with forked tongue
*-)	Stoned
:-T	Tight lipped
:-p	Tongue in cheek

:-&	Tongue tied
:-/	Undecided
:-[	Vampire (1)
:-|<	Vampire (2)
:-<	Vampire (3)
:-)=	Vampire (4)
:-))	Very happy
:-((	Very sad
:-c	Very unhappy
C|:-)	Wearing bowler hat
d:-)	Wearing cap
[:-)	Wearing headphones
:-(#)	Wears teeth braces
;-)	Winking
:-7	Wry smile
|-O	Yawning

Chapter 26

Acronym Dictionary

Wherever you may roam in cyberspace, you will find the footpaths littered with acronyms. TLAs, as they are known, are used in a similar way to smileys. They can help express feelings, giving your text some depth of emotion. TLAs can also be damn useful in cutting down the amount of typing you have to do, becoming a sort of "Virtual Shorthand".

TLA is a TLA itself, being an acronym for Three Letter Acronym. Of course, as is the way of these things, many TLAs have more than three letters (some people call them ETLAs, or Extended Three Letter Acronyms, I call those people a PITA. Look that one up in the TLA Dictionary!). Even more confusing is the fact that many TLAs are not even acronyms at all, but just groups of letters that give a phonetic impression of the phrase implied.

The WDTLAD (that's Wavey Davey TLA Dictionary) is about as complete as you are going to get. I won't say it is comprehensive, I'm far too modest, and there are always new ones being thought up and old ones going out of business. However, with this dictionary next to your computer you should never have to look blankly at your screen wondering just WTF that acronym means again...

Wavey Davey's TLA Dictionary

Acronym	Meaning
AFAICT	As Far As I Can Tell
AFAIK	As Far As I Know
AFK	Away From Keyboard
AIUI	As I Understand It
B4	Before
BAK	Back At Keyboard
BBL	Be Back Later
BCNU	Be seeing you
BRB	Be Right Back
BSF	But Seriously Folks
BST	But Seriously Though
BTDT	Been There Done That

BTSOOM	Beats The Shit Out Of Me
BTW	By The Way
BWQ	Buzz Word Quotient
CLM	Career Limiting Move
CUL	See you later
DWIM	Do What I Mean
DWISNWID	Do What I Say Not What I Do
DYJHIW	Don't You Just Hate It When...
ESAD	Eat Shit And Die
ETLA	Extended Three Letter Acronym
EOF	End Of File
F2F	Face to Face
FAQ	Frequently Asked Question
FFS	For Fucks Sake
FOAD	Fuck Off And Die
FOAF	Friend Of A Friend
FOC	Free Of Charge
FUBAR	Fucked Up Beyond All Recognition
FWIW	For What It's Worth
FYA	For Your Amusement
FYE	For Your Entertainment
FYI	For Your Information
<G>	Grin
GA	Go Ahead
GAL	Get A Life
GIGO	Garbage In Garbage Out
GR&D	Grinning Running & Ducking
HHOJ	Ha Ha, Only Joking
HHOS	Ha Ha, Only Serious
IAE	In Any Event
IANAL	I Am Not A Lawyer
IBN	I'm Buck Naked
IIRC	If I Recall Correctly
IMBO	In My Bloody Opinion
IME	In My Experience
IMHO	In My Humble Opinion
IMNSHO	In My Not So Humble Opinion

IMO	In My Opinion
IOW	In Other Words
IRL	In Real Life
ISTM	It Seems To Me
ISTR	I Seem To Recall
ITRO	In The Region Of
ITRW	In The Real World
IWBNI	It Would Be Nice If
IYSWIM	If You See What I Mean
JAM	Just A Minute
KISS	Keep It Simple, Stupid
L8R	Later
LOL	Laughs Out Loud
MFTL	My Favourite Toy Language
MORF	Male Or Female?
MOTAS	Member Of The Appropriate Sex
MOTOS	Member Of The Opposite Sex
MOTSS	Member Of The Same Sex
MUD	Multi User Dungeon
MUG	Multi User Game
NALOPKT	Not A Lot Of People Know That
NFWM	No Fucking Way Man!
NIFOC	Nude In Front Of Computer
NRN	No Reply Necessary
OAO	Over And Out
OBTW	Oh, By The Way
OEM	Original Equipment Manufacturer
OIC	Oh, I See
OMG	Oh My God
OTOH	On The Other Hand
OTT	Over The Top
PD	Public Domain
PITA	Pain In The Arse
POD	Piece Of Data
RFD	Request For Discussion
ROFL	Rolls On Floor Laughing
RSN	Real Soon Now

RTFAQ	Read The FAQ
RTFM	Read The Fucking Manual
RUOK	Are you OK
SITD	Still In The Dark
SMOP	Small Matter Of Programming
SNAFU	Situation Normal, All Fucked Up
SNR	Signal to Noise Ratio
SO	Significant Other
SOL	Shit Outta Luck
STFU	Shut The Fuck Up
TANSTAAFL	There Ain't No Such Thing As A Free Lunch
TCB	Trouble Came Back
TDM	Too Damn Many
TIA	Thanks In Advance
TIC	Tongue In Cheek
TLA	Three Letter Acronym
TNX	Thanks
TPTB	The Powers That Be
TTFN	Ta Ta For Now
TTYL	Talk To You Later
TVM	Thanks Very Much
UBD	User Brain Damage
VC	Virtual Community
VR	Virtual Reality
WIBNI	Would It Be Nice If
WRT	With Regard To
WTF	What The Fuck
WTH	What The Hell
WYSIWYG	What You See Is What You Get
YABA	Yet Another Bloody Acronym
YHBM	You Have Bin Mail
YHM	You Have Mail

Chapter 27

UNIX command reference

Unless you are already a UNIX junkie you may well find yourself rather confused by all the UNIX commands that litter the Information highways and byeways, but never fear as Wavey Davey is here to help with his compact and bijou UNIX command reference:

>	Directs the output to a file
>>	Appends to a file
<	Directs input from a file
Ctrl/C	Interrupt current process
Ctrl/D	Exit, log out
Ctrl/H	Backspace
Ctrl/J	Terminal reset
Ctrl/S	Stop display scrolling
Ctrl/U	Clear command line
Ctrl/Q	Restart display scrolling
cat	Display file on screen
cd	Change to home directory
cd	Change to specified directory
cdup	Change to previous directory
cp	Copy
grep	Search for text in file
head	Display first few lines of a file
ls	Lists contents of current directory
ls > more	Lists contents of current directory but with the more prompt
mkdir	Create directory
mv	Move
passwd	Change your password
pwd	Prints full pathname of current directory
r	Repeat command
rm	Remove file
rmdir	Remove empty directory
tail	Display last few lines of a file
whoami	Display username

Chapter 28

Glossary

ACK   An acknowledgement number carried in the TCP header that tells a TCP sender the sequence number of the byte which the TCP receiver expects next.

Address   Either the address of a user of a system, as in an email address (required so the message sent can be directed to a particular person) or the address of a site on the Internet.

AFS   A set of protocols, similar to NFS, that allow for the use of files on another network machine as if they were on your local machine.

Analogue Loopback   A modem self test which tests the modem's originate or answer frequency.

Analogue Signals   Continuous but varying waveforms, an example being the voice tones transmitted over a telephone line.

ANSI   American National Standards Institute, responsible for approving standards in many areas.

Anonymous FTP   Anonymous FTP allows a user to retrieve files from another site on the Internet without having to establish a userid and password on the system.

Application   A piece of software that performs a useful function.

Arc   To create a compressed archive of a file, or group of files, using the PKARC compression program. Now very dated, but many arc'ed files are still to be found on the Internet.

Archie   A system for finding publicly available files for FTP over the Internet.

Archive   A file, or group of files, that have been compressed to form one smaller file. Depending on the program used to compress the archive, it will bear one of many file extensions, including .lha .zip .arc .zoo .tar

ARPA   Advanced Research Projects Agency, part of the United States Department of Defence.

ARPAnet   The experimental network upon which the Internet was based.

ARQ   Automatic Repeat Request. An error control protocol used by Miracom modems.

ASCII   American Standard Code for Information Interchange. A code supported by just about every computer manufacturer to represent letters, numbers, and special characters.

Asynchronous   A form of data transmission which allows information to be sent at irregular intervals.

Bandwidth   The difference in Hertz between the highest and lowest frequencies of a transmission channel. Usually used to describe the amount of traffic through a particular newsgroup or conference.

Bang Path   An old UUCP email address system.

Barf   A failure to work!

Baseband   A digital signalling technique used in Ethernet local area networks.

Baud   Unit of measurement denoting the number of transitions in modem signal per second. Each

	transition may carry more than one bit of information.
BBS	Bulletin Board System.
Bigot	A common character type found in Cyberspace.
Bit	A unit of measurement that represents one character of data. A bit is the smallest unit of storage in a computer.
BITNET	An IBM based academic computer network. BITNET is an acronym for "Because It's Time, NETwork"
Bits Per Second	The speed at which bits are transmitted.
Blinking	Using an Off Line Reader to access an online system.
Block	Data consisting of a fixed number of characters or records, moved as a single unit during transmission.
Bogus	Non functional, or not nice.
Bounce	When email is returned due to a failure to deliver.
Bridge	A device that connects two or more physical networks and forwards packets between them.
Broadband	A transmission method often used to send different kinds of signal at the same time, like voice and data for example.
Buffer	A memory area used as a temporary storage device for data during input/output operations.
Byte	A group of binary digits that are stored and operated upon as a unit.

Cable	A bunch of insulated wires with end connectors, an example being a serial cable.
Carrier	A signal of continuous frequency capable of being modulated with another information carrying signal.
CCITT	International Consultative Committee for Telegraphy and Telephony. An organisation that produces international technical standards for data communications. Has recently been replaced by the ITU-T.
Cello	A World Wide Web graphical browser program for Windows users.
Character	A binary representation of a letter, number or symbol.
CIM	The CompuServe Information Manager is the officially supported off line reader and system navigator for CompuServe.
CI$	See also "CIS". The dollar sign replaces the "S" in this slang version, due to the cost of using the service.
CIS	CompuServe, the American online information service.
Cix	Compulink Information eXchange. The largest conferencing system in the UK.
Cix	The Commercial Internet Exchange, an agreement amongst Internet Service Providers regarding the commercial use of the Internet. Not to be confused with the Compulink Information eXchange although it quite often is as they share the same acronym.

CIXen	People who use the Compulink Information eXchange.
Client	An application that extracts information from a server on your behalf.
CommUnity	The Computer Communicators Association, set up to protect and further computer communications in the UK. Similar in aims to the EFF, but with a UK perspective.
COM	A code in MS-DOS that refers to a serial port.
Compress	A UNIX archiving program that "compresses" the size of a file.
Conference	A message area, or forum, on a conferencing system like Cix. Each conference covers a defined subject matter, and is further subdivided into topics of more specific subject matter. For example, there may be a sooty conference which has topics of sooty, sweep, and sue.
Connect Time	The length of time you spend on-line to the Internet.
Cookie	A random quote, generated by software. Found on many online systems.
CoSy	CoSy is the operating system that online services like Cix and BIX are based upon. It is a shortening of the words "Conferencing System".
CPS	Characters Per Second. A measurement of data output speed.
Crash	A sudden and total system failure.

CRC	Cyclic Redundancy Checking. A type of error detection.
CREN	The Corporation for Research and Educational Networking, which was formed by a merger of BITNET and CSNET.
Cross post	To post the same message to more than one conference, message area, newsgroup.
CTS	Clear To Send, an RS-232C signal that basically means that everything is OK for transmission of data.
Cyberpunk	A person who "lives" in the future culture of Cyberspace, Virtual Reality etc. As epitomised by the works of Bruce Sterling.
Cyberspace	A term coined by William Gibson in his novel "Neuromancer" used to describe the collective "World" of networked computers. Now commonly used to refer to the world that exists within computer networks, accessed by comms technology. My favourite definition is simply "the electric domain".
Daemon	A program which sits on a system waiting to automatically perform a specific function. Daemon is an acronym for "Disk and Execution MONitor".
DARPA	The Defence Advanced Research Projects Agency, responsible for the development of ARPANET which was the basis of what was to develop into the Internet.
DASD	Direct Access Storage Device.

Data Compression	The compression of information to decrease transferred file size. MNP5 and V.42bis are the best known types.
Datagram	The primary unit of information transferred over the Internet using the Internet Protocol.
DCE	Data Communications Equipment.
Decryption	Decoding encrypted data to its original form.
Dial-Up	To connect to another computer by calling it over the telephone network.
DIP Switch	Dual Interface Poll switch which enables the user to set various parameters of a circuit board (commonly found on modems and printers).
DNS	Domain Name System is a database system for translating computer domain names into numeric Internet addresses.
Domain	Part of the naming hierarchy of the Internet.
Domain Name Server	Domain Name Servers enable domain names to be resolved into numerical IP addresses.
Down	Not working, as in "the BBS is down".
Download	The transfer of a file from another, remote, computer to your computer.
DTE	Data Terminal Equipment.
DTR	Data Terminal Ready, an RS-232C signal that is part of the handshake in a data transmission interface.

Duplex	A communications channel capable of carrying a signal in both directions.
EARN	European Academic Research Network.
EFF	Electronic Frontier Foundation, an American organisation that addresses the social and legal issues arising from the increased use of computer communications.
EMACS	One of the most common editors found on online systems.
Email	Electronic Mail. A method of sending messages via computer instead of the usual land based postal system. One of the most popular and important uses of computer communications.
Emote Icons	See "smiley".
Encryption	A method of coding data to prevent unathorised access, most commonly used on the Internet to protect email from prying eyes.
Equalisation	A compensation circuit built into some modems to offset distortion caused by the telephone channel.
Error Control	A variety of different techniques which check the reliability of characters or blocks of data.
Ethernet	A type of high speed local area network.
EUNet	European UNIX Network.
FAQ	A Frequently Asked Question. You will find FAQ files all over the Internet, in Usenet Newsgroups, mailing

lists, at FTP, Gopher, and WWW sites. You'll even find a FAQ section in this book!

File Server   A computer that stores files on the Internet, making them available for access by various Internet tools.

Finger   A program that displays the user, or users, on a remote system.

Firewall   A firewall is a security device to help protect a private network from Internet crackers and hackers. It is a machine with two network interfaces that is configured to restrict what protocols can be used across the boundaries and to decide what internal IP addresses can be seen to the external Internet.

Flame   An abusive or personal attack against the poster of a message. A flame is the online equivalent of losing your rag or thumping your teapot.

Flow Control   A technique to compensate for the differences in the flow of data input and output from a modem.

Fortune Cookie   See "Cookie".

Forum   A message area on CompuServe or Delphi,, equivalent to an echo on Fidonet, a newsgroup on USENET, or a conference on CIX.

Fragmentation   The process by which an IP datagram is broken into smaller pieces, so as to meet the requirements of a specific physical network.

Frame   A block of data with header and trailer information attached.

FreeNet	A popular method of providing "free" access to the Internet from the United States. Probably the most famous being the Cleveland FreeNet, which was also the first.
FTP	The File Transfer Protocol that defines how files are transferred over the Internet.
Full Duplex	Flow of information in both directions at the same time.
Gateway	A computer system to transfer data between otherwise incompatible networks.
Gibson, William	Author of "Neuromancer". Responsible for coining the term "Cyberspace".
Gopher	A menu based system for exploring the Internet.
Hacker	Someone who enjoys exploring computer systems, often applied to people who undertake such explorations illegally.
Half Duplex	Flow of information in both directions, but one way at a time.
Handshaking	An exchange of signals allowing communication between two devices, designed to start or keep the two in synchronisation.
Hayes	A modem manufacturer responsible for the first direct connection modems, and whose command set has become the industry standard.
Header	Part of a packet which precedes the actual data and contains source, destination, and error checking information.

Host	A computer that allows users to communicate with other computers on a network.
Hostname	The name given to a host computer.
HST	High Speed Technology. A proprietary signalling scheme used as part of the trademark for Miracom HST modems.
HTML	HyperText Mark-up Language, the language used to write a World Wide Web document.
HTTP	HyperText Transfer Protocol, used extensively by World Wide Web. Another of the many Internet protocols.
Hub	A device connected to many other devices.
Hz	Hertz. A measurement of frequency, each unit being one cycle per second.
IAB	The Internet Architecture Board, if you like the "head honchos" who make decisions about Internet standards.
ICMP	Internet Control Message Protocol is the group of messages exchanged by IP modules in order to report errors.
Internet	Worldwide network of computer networks, connected using the IP protocol.
Internet Society	An organisation that exists to support the Internet, and also the governing body of the Internet Architecture Board.
IP	Internet Protocol on which the Internet is based.

IRC	Internet Relay Chat allows many users to chat in real time across the Internet.
ISDN	Integrated Services Digital Network combines voice and digital network services in one medium.
ISN	Initial Sequence Number is the first sequence number used on a TCP connection.
ITU-T	International Telecommunications UnionTelecommunications. The Telecommunications standards making organisation, which replaces the CCITT.
JANET	The Joint Academic NETwork of educational establishments in the UK.
JUNET	Japanese UNIX Network.
KA9Q	An implementation of TCP/IP for amateur packet radio systems.
Kermit	A file transfer protocol named after Kermit the Frog!
Kernel	The system commands containing level of an operating system or network system.
Kill File	A file which filters out any messages posted by those people named in it. If someone is in your kill file, you never see any messages from them again, hence you have effectively killed them. Seen in great numbers on Usenet but also implemented in a growing number of Off Line Readers for various online systems.
Kit	Computer equipment.

Knowbot	The Knowbot Information Service is another method of trying to find where someone dwells within the Internet.
LAN	Local Area Network, a data network that serves a small area only.
Leased Line	A permanent connection between two sites, which requires no voltage on the line and no dialling.
LED	Light Emitting Diode. A device that emits light when electrical voltage is applied to it. Used on modem front panels as status indicators.
Line Noise	Disruption of computer communications caused by interference on the telephone line.
Lion Nose	See "line noise",
LISTSERV	An automated mailing list distribution system.
Local Echo	All transmitted data is sent to the screen of the sending computer.
Log	A record of file operations. In comms use, the storing to disk or file of an on-line session.
Login	The process of identifying yourself on an online system. Generally a two stage process involving the input of your username followed by your password.
Login Name	The "username" or name of your account used for identification purposes.
Lurker	Someone who reads but doesn't post in newsgroups, conferences, or message areas. A sort of online voyeur.

Macro	A macro instruction is a string or instruction replaced by a shorter string or instruction. In use this means you can execute a long sequence by typing just a short one.
Mail Gateway	A machine that transfers mail between two or more email systems.
Mailing List	A discussion group whose messages are distributed by email.
MHS	Message Handling System.
MILNET	The US MILitary NETwork.
MIME	Mulitpurpose Internet Mail Extensions, a method of linking binary code into email.
MNP	Microcom Network Protocol is a common modem error correction system.
Mode	A specific condition or state under which a device may operate.
Modem	MOdulator/DEModulator. A device to convert binary information into an analogue signal that can be transmitted over normal voice carrying telephone lines, and convert that signal back into computer readable data at the other end.
Moderator	The person who runs, or moderates, a conference or message area.
Mosaic	Probably the most commonly used World Wide Web graphical browser. Has been developed for many platforms, including Windows, Amiga, X-Windows, and Macintosh.

MTU	Maximum Transmission Unit is the largest unit of data that can be sent on a given system.
MUD	Multi User Dungeon, an online role playing adventure game.
MUG	Multi User Game, any online game where there are two or more players at the same time.
Net	Generally used as another name for the Internet, although sometimes people refer to both USENET and Cyberspace in general as "The Net".
Netfind	A service that helps find email addresses for people on the Internet.
Net God	Someone who has achieved a "Godlike" status on the Net, either through the development of part of the Net or tools used in it, or because of their presence on the Net.
Net Police	A derogatory term applied to those people who feel it is their duty to tell others how they should behave in Cyberspace.
Net Surfer	Someone who "surfs" the Internet, wandering around looking for interesting places to visit, interesting files to grab, and interesting people to talk to.
Netiquette	The supposed etiquette of the online community, examples being avoiding overuse of quoting, avoiding cross posting, and so on.
Network	A group of computers that can communicate with each other.

Newbie	Someone who is a newcomer to a USENET group, often used as a term of ridicule or abuse.
Newsgroup	A message area, defined by subject matter, which forms part of USENET.
NFS	The Network File System, allows use of files on remote network machines as if they were one your local machine.
NIC	Network Information Centre.
Node	A computer attached to a network.
NRAM	Non-volatile memory used by such devices as modems to store a user definable configuration which is read and acted upon at power up.
NSFNET	The National Science Foundation Network is one of the networks that makes up the Internet.
Null Modem	A cable used to directly connect two computers by their serial ports in which the transmitting and receiving pins are swapped.
Numeric Database	A database containing, specifically and unsurprisingly, numbers.
Offline	Not connected to an online system.
Off Line Reader	See "OLR".
OLR	Off Line Reader, a program that enables you to connect to an online system, download all your messages and Email, read and reply to the offline and then send back your replies. An OLR can save you lots of money in telephone bills and online service

charges, as well as provide in some cases a better user interface to the online system.

On-line
Refers to when two computers are connected by means of modems. For example, a Bulletin Board System is also an Online System.

Originate Mode
When the modem transmits in frequencies which are the reverse of the modem being called which is in answer mode.

Packet
A bundle of data.

Parity Bit
A check bit added to a unit of data for error checking purposes.

Password
A security string that is required to be input before access to a system, or part of a system, may be granted.

Phreaking
Making phone calls whilst bypassing the charging system. Phone phreaking was the forerunner to hacking as we understand it today.

PING
Packet Internet Groper is a program used to test destinations on the Internet to see if they exist, are operating, etc.

Plonk
The sound a newbie makes as he plummets to the bottom of a killfile list in a USENET group.

Pointer
A file marker so that an online system can remember what messages you have read when you disconnect, so you don't have to read them all again next time.

Polling
Connecting to another system to check for email and messages etc.

Port Number	Computers which run the TCP/IP protocols can use different ports to run different services. Each of these ports is allocated a specific number. Local services tend to be assigned on higher port numbers.
Post	To send a message, either by email or to a conference, message area, or newsgroup.
Postmaster	The person responsible for taking care of mail across the Internet.
PPP	Point to Point Protocol. This allows a computer to use TCP/IP with a standard telephone line.
Profile	A control file for a program. Most commonly used to set up a users individual preferences when logging onto an online service.
Protocol	Standards governing the transfer of information between computers. Developed to improve the reliability and speed of data transfer.
Public Domain	Software which is available to anyone without the requirement to pay for it.
Remote Echo	Everything the remote computer transmits is duplicated on your computers screen.
REN	Ring Equivalent Number refers to a total figure which must not be surpassed by equipment connected to a single telephone socket.
REN and STIMPY	Happy Happy, Joy Joy.
Resume	A text file containing personal information about a user of an online system, usually written by the user themselves.

RFC	Request For Comments are sets of papers used for discussion on Internet standards.
ROT-13	A simple form of encryption, commonly applied to some USENET messages, which rotates the alphabet 13 places forwards or backwards.
Router	A system that transfers information between two networks using the same protocols.
Scratchpad	A temporary file used to hold messages whilst awaiting transfer or editing. Used on some online systems such as CIX.
Serial Cable	The cable used to connect devices through a computer's serial port.
Serial Port	The port that transmits and receives asynchronous data. Peripheral devices such as modems, printers, and mice can all use the serial port.
Server	A computer, or the software on that computer, that allows other computers to use it by means of client software.
Service Provider	Any organisation offering connections to the Internet, or part of it.
Shareware	Software which is generally available as "try before you buy" with the available version needing to be registered before its full power can be unleashed.
SIG	Special Interest Group, a forum or collection of forums on a particular subject. Found on on-line systems such as Delphi and CompuServe.

Signal to noise ratio Used to describe the amount of on topic postings as compared to the amount of wibble within a message area or conference.

Signature A personal tag line used on the end of messages posted to online services. These can vary from a couple of words to many lines long. Also known commonly as "sigs".

Site Any of the individual networks that, as a whole, comprise the Internet.

SLIP Serial Line IP is a protocol that allows a computer to use the Internet protocols using a standard telephone line.

Smiley A smiling face character made by joining ASCII characters together. Used to express emotions etc. See the "Smiley Dictionary" in this book for more details.

SMTP Simple Mail Transfer Protocol is used to transfer email between computers, as part of the TCP/IP protocol family.

Snail Mail The sending of mail using the traditional land based postal system as opposed to email. So called because of its slowness compared to electronic mail.

Start/Stop Bits Bits attached to a character before transmission during an asynchronous transfer.

Sterling, Bruce Author mainly responsible for the coining of the term "Cyberpunk".

SysOp SYStem OPerator, the person who runs a Bulletin Board System.

TCP	Transmission Control Protocol, one of the protocols upon which the Internet is based.
Teapot	One of my favourite words.
Teledildonics	The sexual act performed with the aid of Virtual Reality, computers, telecommunications and a couple of very sad and lonley people indeed.
Telnet	An Internet protocol that allows you to log in to other computer systems on the Net.
Thread	A series of postings to a message area or conference that are linked together. A thread consists of an initial posting followed by all the comments to it, and forms an online conversation or debate.
Throughput	The amount of data transmitted per second without the overhead of protocol information.
TLA	A Three Letter Acronym, although these are often found to contain more than three letters. Used to minimise typing and speed up communications. See the "TLA Dictionary" in this book for more details.
Topic	A subdivision of a conference, where the subject matter has been more distinctly defined. See entry for "conference" for more details.
UDP	User Datagram Protocol, another of the protocols upon which the Internet is based.
UNIX	An operating system commonly used across the Internet.
Upload	The sending of a file from your computer to another, remote, computer.

URL	Uniform Resource Locator, an attempt to standardise the location or address details of Internet resources. Most commonly used, at the moment, in connection with the World Wide Web.
USENET	A group of systems that exchange debate, chat, etc in the form of newsgroups across the Internet.
UUCP	Unix to Unix copy is used for copying files between unix systems.
UUencode	A method of encoding binary data so that it can be sent as an ASCII file across networks by email. A decoder is required to convert the file back into an executable binary file again.
V.21	An ITU-T standard, a modem speed of 300bps
V.22	An ITU-T standard, a modem speed of 1200bps
V.22bis	An ITU-T standard, a modem speed of 2400bps
V.23	An ITU-T standard, sending data at 75bps and receiving data at 1200bps
V.32	An ITU-T standard, a modem speed of 9600bps
V.32bis	An ITU-T standard, a modem speed of 14400bps
V.34	An ITU-T standard a modem speed of 28800bps
V.42	An ITU-T error correction standard
V.42bis	An ITU-T error correction standard with data compression

All you need to know about the Internet

Veronica
An Internet tool that provides a Gopher menu that matched your keyword Gopher search.

Video Display
A monitor to those not talking techno-babble Terminal

Virtual Circuit
A logical transmission path.

Virtuai Communities
A term that describes the communities that are very real, but exist only in computer networks. Another name for Cyberspace.

Virtual Reality
A computer technology that creates a very real illusion of being in an artificial world. Virtual Reality has already found its way into many real-life applications, from chemistry to architecture to games.

Virus
A program designed to infect and sometimes destroy other programs and computer equipment. Virus programmers are known, politely, as SMEEEEEEEEEEEEEEGHEADS.

WAIS
Wide Area Information Servers are used for searching databases across the Internet.

WAN
A Wide Area Network as opposed to a Local Area Network.

White Pages
A list of Internet users, accessible through the Internet itself.

Whois
An Internet program to find out the email address etc of someone from agiven name.

Wibble
Nonsense posted to a message area, conference, or newsgroup. Made into an art form by the likes of

talk.bizarre on USENET and the norman conference on CIX.

World Wide Web   A hypertext based information and resource system for the Internet.

WWW   See "World Wide Web".

X.25   A packet switched data network, which is usually half-duplex.

X.29   The command set used to configure and establish X.25 connections.

X.400   An ITU-T standard for Email formats.

Zip   To archive a file or group of files using the PKZip archiver.

Index

.net All you need to know about the Internet

All you need to know about the Internet **.net**

Other books from
Future Publishing

Copies of the following books for PC owners are available direct from **Future Publishing Limited, Freepost (BS4900) Somerton, Somerset, TA11 6BR.** They are also available in all good bookshops. Retailers can order copies from our distributors, Computer Bookshops, on 021 706 1250.

All you need to know imprint

The aim of the imprint is to cover the software features most users use most of the time, enabling the reader to get up and running as quickly as possible. These books assume a familiarity with the Windows environment, and all are written with a series of helpful icons highlighting important information. They are written with a walk-through tutorial style, and make extensive use of illustrations and screen grabs. All these books are suitable for both beginners and intermediate users

All you need to know about PCs
by Geoff Oakshott
ISBN 1-85870-055-8
Pages 350
Size 220mm (H) x 150mm (W)
Publication Date October 1994
Order no. FBB0558
The first book of the 'All you need to know' imprint, is an introduction to PC's and also includes hints and tips suitable for the more experienced user. It includes an introduction to computing – the hardware and software, the operating systems and much more – and all in plain English. If you haven't bought your PC yet this books tells you what to look out for, if you have, it'll make it work for you.

All you Need to Know about WordPerfect 6.0a for Windows
by Stephen Copestake
ISBN 1-85870-056-6
Pages 320
Size 220mm (H) x 150mm (W)
Publication Date November 1994
Order no. FBB0566

Covers version 6.0 of the program with the added refinements included in the interim release 6.0a. As well as providing a complete insight into WordPerfect 6.0 for Windows, the book provides a quick check list of all the new features for those upgrading from previous versions.

All you Need to Know about Excel 5.0 for Windows
by Stephen Copestake
ISBN 1-85870-057-4
Pages 320
Size 220mm (H) x 150mm (W)
Publication Date November 1994
Order no. FBB0574
This book takes a jargon-free look at Excel 5.0 for Windows – it covers the features which most users use, most of the time. Icons draw your attention to useful hints, tips and key techniques, while the tutorial style and liberal use of illustrations lets you gain a thorough understanding of the software in the shortest possible time.

All you Need to Know about Lotus 1-2-3 (versions 4.0 & 5.0) for Windows
by Ian Sinclair
ISBN 1-85870-058-2
Pages 300
Size 220mm (H) x 150mm (W)
Publication Date October 1994
Order no. FBB0582
The book covers all the main elements of this leading spreadsheet package including its often unexploited data handling capabilities. In order to keep you up to date with all the latest developments the book includes all the refinements of the latest release, version 5.0.

All you Need to Know about CD-ROM
by Damien Noonan
ISBN 1-85870-059-0
Pages 350
Dimensions 230mm x 185mm
Publication Date November 1994

All you need to know about the Internet

Order no. FBB0590
From the publishers of CD-ROM Today magazine, written by the launch
editor, Damien Noonan. CD ROM has finally emerged as the way forward
for computing, this book provides a comprehensive insight into the
technology and its applications.

Money Management imprint

Money Management with Quicken 6.0 for DOS
by Jean Miles
ISBN 1-85870-012-4
Pages 230
Dimensions 205mm x 120mm
Price £8.95
Publication Date May 1994
Order no. FBB0124
Now into its third print run the book has enjoyed success exceeded only by
the software sales and is every bit a best-seller. It provides a comprehensive
guide to all the facilities of Intuit's DOS version of this leading finance
package.

Money Management with Quicken 3.0 for Windows
by Jean Miles
ISBN 1-85870-017-5
Dimensions 220mm x 150mm
Price £12.95
Pages 280
Publication date April 1994
Order no. FBB0175
The second Quicken book from the pen of Jean Miles, this book has the
Official backing of the software publishers, Intuit Software and is a
comprehensive look at this latest release of Quicken. This book is already
established on the path to best-seller status.

Money Management with Sage Moneywise 2.0 for Windows
by Jean Miles

ISBN 1-85870-043-4
Dimensions 220mm x 150mm
Price £12.95
Pages 250
Publication date October 1994
Order no. FBB 0434
The third Money Management book from Jean Miles. It covers all the features of SageSoft's entry level package Moneywise. As with all the Money Management books it has the full endorsement of the software developers Sage.

Money Management with Microsoft Money 3.0 for Windows
by Andrew Marlow
ISBN 1-85870-044-2
Dimensions 220mm x 150mm
Price £12.95
Pages 280
Publication date November 1994
Order no. FBB 0442
The fourth book of the imprint, written for Microsoft's latest version of their personal accounting package, Money 3.0.

Professional imprint

The Complete Desktop Publishing Guidebook
by Simon Williams & Geoffrey Oakshott
ISBN 1-85870-003-5
Pages 470
Dimensions 235mm x 185mm
Price £24.95
Publication date October 1994
Order no. FBB 0035
A thorough insight into desktop publishing and design. This book provides advice and guidance on how to use dtp as an effective business tool. From the Publishers of PC Plus magazine.

All you need to know about the Internet **.net** the internet magazine

Successful Business Accounting with Sage Sterling +2 Version 2
by Andrew Marlow
ISBN 1-85870-013-2
Pages 300
Dimensions 235mm x 185mm
Price £24.95
Publication date June 1994
Order no. FBB0132
A comprehensive look at the Sage +2 range of business products which comes complete with a free, complete copy of the Bank Interest Calculator software direct from Sage UK, with a number of business templates produced by the author. The latest officially endorsed books from Future Publishing.

The Complete Access Workbook
by Arthur Tennick
ISBN 1-85870-011-6
Pages 250
Dimensions 223mm x 190mm
Price £17.95
Publication date May 1994
Order no. FBB 0116
A comprehensive database package requires something similar from a book. The Complete Access Workbook provides something for every type of user whether an absolute beginner or a professional programmer. It will guide you through the process of designing your database.

The Modem and Communications Guidebook
by Sue Schofield
ISBN 1-85870-000-0
Pages 350
Dimensions 235mm x 185mm
Price £19.95
Publication date November 1993
Order no. FBB0000
Written and researched in the UK, this book makes communications easy to learn, productive and trouble-free. Clear explanations of all the basic ideas

without the unnecessary jargon, make the process of going on-line painless and straightforward. This book has very quickly established itself as a best seller and includes free comms software and Cix subscription.

Windows 3.1 HelpScreen
by Arthur Tennick
ISBN 1-85870-001-9
Pages 350
Dimensions 223mm x 190mm
Price £19.95
Publication date November 1993
Order no. FBB0019
Provides the straight forward answers to all the questions you might have about Windows - this book is for those with a basic familiarity with Windows but who wish to progress and quickly build their expertise. With a wealth of Windows books available it is reassuring to know you have the hallmark of authority from the UK's leading PC magazine PC Plus.

The PC Plus HelpScreen Collection
by Barry Thomas
ISBN 1-85870-002-7
Pages 150
Dimensions 240mm x 205mm
Price £14.95 (includes disk)
Publication date October 1993
Order no. FBB0027
A compilation of the last two years of HelpScreen pages within PC Plus. All material has been edited and rewritten to provide accessible time-saving information.

The Software Guide
Pages 450
Dimensions 240mm x170mm
Price £24.95
Publication date March 1994
Order no. PSG003
The authoritative new directory of IBM-compatible PC software, this book
comes to you from the publishers of Britain's best selling PC magazine, PC
Plus. It provides details of more than 3000 software products including
hardware requirements, price and feature analysis.

Future Books Priority Order Form

You can use this tear-off coupon to order any of the Future Publishing books described on the previous pages. Simply fill in the details in the spaces provided and post your coupon, together with payment, in an envelope to the following address:

Future Book Orders, Future Publishing Ltd, Freepost (BS4900), Somerton, Somerset TA11 6BR

Your name _____

Your address _____

_____ Postcode_____

Your signature _____

now turn over

 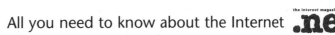

Please send me (tick as appropriate):

	Title	Code	Price
☐	All you need to know about PCs	FBB0558	£14.95
☐	All you need to know about WordPerfect 6.0a for Windows	FBB0566	£12.95
☐	All you need to know about Excel 5.0 for Windows	FBB0574	£12.95
☐	All you need to know about Lotus 1-2-3 (versions 4.0 & 5.0) for Windows	FBB0582	£12.95
☐	All you need to know about CD-ROM	FBB0590	£14.95
☐	All you need to know about the Internet	FBB0647	£14.95
☐	Money Management with Quicken 6.0 for DOS	FBB0124	£8.95
☐	Money Management with Quicken 3.0 for Windows	FBB0175	£12.95
☐	Money Management with Sage Moneywise 2.0 for Windows	FBB0434	£12.95
☐	Money Management with Microsoft Money 3.0 for Windows	FBB0442	£12.95
☐	The Complete Desktop Publishing Guidebook	FBB0035	£24.95
☐	Successful Business Accounting with Sage Sterling +2 Version 2	FBB0132	£24.95
☐	The Complete Access Workbook	FBB0116	£17.95
☐	The Modem and Communications Guidebook	FBB0000	£19.95
☐	Windows 3.1 HelpScreen	FBB0019	£19.95
☐	The PC Plus HelpScreen Collection	FBB0027	£14.95
☐	The Software Guide	PSG003	£24.95

Amount enclosed £   (Make cheques payable to Future Publishing Ltd.)

Method of payment (tick one): VISA ☐ ACCESS ☐ CHEQUE ☐ POSTAL ORDER ☐

CARD NUMBER ☐☐☐☐ ☐☐☐☐ ☐☐☐☐ ☐☐☐☐

EXPIRY DATE ☐☐ ☐☐

Tick if you do not wish to receive direct mail from other companies ☐

Now send this form and your payment to the address on the front of this coupon. **You will not need a stamp when you post this order and postage and packing are free. There are no extra costs.** Please allow 28 days for delivery.   **AYNINT**

the internet magazine
.net All you need to know about the Internet

Other Internet books
Future Publishing

To accompany 'All you need to know about the Internet' and in conjunction with .net magazine there is a whole series of books under the '.net Guide' imprint. Each consists of between 150-200 pages, is sized at 220mm (H) x 150mm (W) and retails at £7.95.

.net Guide #1   All you need to know about **Getting On-Line**
by Toby Simpson
How to get on the Net quickly, easily and cheaply. No nonsense, no jargon, no hassle.
ISBN 1-898275-31-9
Publication Date November 1994

.net Guide #2   All you need to know about **Communicating On-Line**
by Davey Winder
Do you know 3 million people? You do now. Find out how to talk to people all over the world.
ISBN 1-898275-32-7
Publication Date November 1994

.net Guide #3   All you need to know about **Using the Net**
by Davey Winder
The Net software is your gateway to a world of information. Find out how to really use it.
ISBN 1-898275-33-5
Publication Date November 1994

.net Guide #4   All you need to know about **Teleworking**
by Gus Chandler
No commuting, no rush-hour… no boss? Find out how to work from home via the Net.
ISBN 1-898275-34-3
Publication Date November 1994

.net Guide #5   All you need to know about **On-Line Information**
by Gus Chandler
Forget your local library. The Net is the biggest source of information the
world has ever seen. Find out how to get it.
ISBN 1-898275-35-1
Publication Date January 1995

.net Guide #6   All you need to know about **Mailing Lists**
by Davey Winder
Don't go searching for information – make it come to you. Keep up to date
on anything from poodles to particle accelerators.
ISBN 1-898275-36-X
Publication Date January 1995

.net Guide #7   All you need to know about **Setting up a BBS**
by Toby Simpson
Find out how to run your own on-line service. What it costs, what to avoid –
and how to make it a success.
ISBN 1-898275-37-8
Publication Date January 1995

net Guide #8   All you need to know about **On-Line Gaming**
by Davey Winder
Games consoles are history. Discover real gaming with real people in real
situations. On-line gaming is the future.
ISBN 1-898275-38-6
Publication Date January 1995

.net Guide #9 All you need to know about **UK Internet Service Providers**
by Davey Winder
You need a Service Provider. Find out who offers what and for how much.
ISBN 1-898275-39-4
Publication Date January 1995

All you need to know about the Internet **.net**
the internet magazine

.net Guide #10   All you need to know about **The World Wide Web**
by Davey Winder
Compare colour TV with long-wave radio. That's the WorldWide Web
compared to the standard Net interface. Believe it.
ISBN 1-898275-40-8
Publication Date January 1995

.net Guide #11   All you need to know about **Business On-Line**
by Davey Winder
Good business is all about communication, expertise and commercial
awareness. Find out how the Net will give you the edge.
ISBN 1-898275-42-4
Publication Date February 1995

.net Guide #12   Ali you need to know about **Internet jargon**
by Davey Winder
Baffled by jargon? Hacked off with technical terms? Every Internet buzz-
word is explained right here. In plain English.
ISBN 1-898275-43-2
Publication Date February 1995

To find out the latest on availability and prices, call our order hotline

☎ 01225 822511

Special offers

Over the next few pages you'll find special offers on on-line subscriptions and services, hardware and software. Together, they could save you the cost of this book many times over!

Pace MobiFax 144
– portable fax and data modem

14400bps for only £105*

- ○ quick and easy to use
- ○ includes everything you need to get connected
- ○ high speed fax and data communications
- ○ free fax and communications software
- ○ free connection to CompuServe and Almac BBS
- ○ 5 year warranty

Available to all readers of 'All you need to know about the Internet' direct from:

Misco Computer Supplies (UK) Ltd, Faraday Close, Park Farm Industrial Estate, Wellingborough, Northants. NN8 6XH. Tel: 01933 400 400

Quote product reference 21115 with your credit card details

*price excludes VAT at 17.5% and £7.45 next day delivery

Internet in a Bag

New Internet Chameleon is the foremost professional access software for surfing the web, with a huge variety of state-of-the-art tools including Websurfer, Gopher and full email with MIME. Special upgrade prices are available for readers of '**All you need to know about the Internet**'.

Leaf's new Internet Access service, SERVELAN, gives you full, unrestricted access to the Internet via a network of POPs across the UK and Europe… even on the move you can keep in touch.

Add to this a PACE modem from our high-quality range, support from our helpful and committed team, wrap it all up and there you have it…
Internet in a Bag!

Call us NOW for details of our amazing upgrade prices and of the special bagged deals we offer!

**(Internet Chameleon + Servelan + PACE)
= Internet in a Bag**

from Leaf Distribution Limited…

7 Elmwood, Chineham Business Park, Crockford Lane, Basingstoke RG24 0WG. Telephone 01256 707777. Fax 01256 707555 email sales@leaf.co.uk

All you need to know about the Internet **.net** the internet magazine

Free registration to The Direct Connection

The Direct Connection allows users to access all of the popular Internet services and many other unique services besides, from a simple to use menu driven system. They are offering readers of 'All you need to know about the Internet' free registration to their 'Enhanced Login' accounts when they sign up using the online demonstration service.

1   Dial 081 317 2222 using a terminal emulation package set to 8 bits, no parity, 1 stop bit.

2   When prompted log in as 'demo'

3   Readers must enter the title of this book when asked where they heard about The Direct Connection

Offer expires 31/12/95

Free introductory CompuServe membership

When you connect your computer to CompuServe, you are joining one of the world's largest networks of people with personal computers. You will have access to more than 2 million members and over 2,000 services that offer a source of technical support, business information, entertainment and communications. Free introductory membership includes:

- Your first month's membership free (worth approx £6*)
- A $15 (£10*) introductory usage credit to explore CompuServe's extended services
- A copy of the CompuServe Information Manager software for Windows
- A mini users guide
- Freephone support 9am - 9pm Monday - Friday and 10am - 5pm Saturdays
- A complimentary subscription to CompuServe Magazine, CompuServe's monthly computing publication

Start connecting to CompuServe by calling 0800 289378 and quote this reference: "REP 824"

*CompuServe is a worldwide service but is priced in US dollars. Billing is in local currency at the prevailing rate of exchange.

Offer expires 31/12/95

All you need to know about the Internet

Try the Internet free for five hours* with Delphi

Delphi Internet makes it easy to get on-line!

- No joining fee
- Immediate access with Visa/MasterCard
- Service plans from only £10 a month**
- Choice of fast, menu-driven interface (suitable for PC, Mac, Amiga) or free Windows interface
- No surcharges for fast modems
- No surcharges for Internet mail
- No surcharges for time of day

Delphi Internet gives you the Internet and much more!

- Full Internet access – gophers, FTP, WWW, thousands of newsgroups, mail and telnet access to millions of computers
- Full access to UK Delphi – with unique services including Davey Winder's own forum, media services from The Times, Sunday Times, Sky News and more
- Full access to US Delphi – with exciting games like Air Warrior***, news from Reuters, hundreds of special forums, thousands of downloadables.

To get on-line right now...

1   Set your modem to 8-1-N and dial 0171 284 2424
2   On connection enter @D <return> (this will not appear on the screen as you type it)
3   At the username prompt enter GODELPHI <return>
4   At the password prompt enter FUTURE <return>

*   Five hours in the calendar month of joining are free: after you have tried the service, you can choose the membership plan that suits you best, or cancel with no obligation.
**   All prices exclude VAT
***   Air Warrior surcharged at 54p an hour

Delphi Internet Ltd, The Elephant House, Hawley Crescent, London NW1 8NP. For further information, **phone** 0171 757 7080, **fax** 0171 757 7160 or email **UK@DELPHI.COM**

the internet magazine
.net All you need to know about the Internet

Free registration to Cix

Now you can access the world of the Internet, email and online conferencing at a saving of £25. Cix is the UK's largest computer conferencing service, offering a wide range of services including:

- Full Internet Access
- Full email facilities
- Over 5,000 on-line conferences
- Usenet, IRC and Gopher

For further information about the range of services Cix provides, or for a free information pack, please phone the Customer Care line on 0492 641 961. To register free, all you need to do is:

1   Use your modem and comms software to dial up 081 390 1244 (or 081 390 1255 if busy)
2   Type CIX at the Login: prompt
3   At the Nickname: prompt type new
4   After entering your details, you will be asked if you have a special code. Type y (for yes), and when asked what the special code is simply enter futurebook to save £25!

Cut-price modem & software bundle

SEG Communications have put together a special hardware/software bundle only for readers of 'All you need to know about the Internet'. The bundle comprises:

- US Robotics Sportster 14.4 Fax Modem (RRP £199) complete with QuickLink Comms/Fax software
- SC5500 High Speed Serial Card for PC (RRP £30) – essential for reliable high-speed comms under Windows.

Offer price £139 (+ carriage and VAT)

Payment can be made by cheque or credit card. SEG Communications offer after-sales support and are happy to discuss individual queries before or after purchase.

SEG Communications, 137 Hale Lane, Edgware, Middlesex HA8 9QP. Tel: 0181 959 3377. Fax: 0181 959 2137. Email: segcom@cix.compulink.co.uk

Offer subject to availability and change without notice. Sales subject to SEG's standard terms of trading. Offer expires 31st January 1994 – please call for pricing after that time. Please make cheques payable to SEG Communications.

Cut-price subscription to Easynet

Save £10

Easynet, the full Internet access providers, give you all you will ever need to get the most from the Internet. Email, Usenet, FTP, Gopher, Archie, WWW, IRC and more. You can save £10 on the joining fee as a reader of this book.

For further details, call 0171 209 0990 quoting the reference "DW94"

MicroPrism (UK) Limited, 178-202 Great Portland Street, London.

Email **mprism@easynet.co.uk**

All you need to know about the Internet **.net** the internet magazine

CityScape IP-GOLD
Getting out there made easy

The unique introduction to the Information Highway

NO EXPERIENCE REQUIRED

- Easy to install in less than ten minutes
- Backed up by experts on hand for full user support
- Professional quality product

- IP-GOLD is the ultimate EASY-TO-USE Internet Conductivity service
- IP-GOLD provides graphical software as easy to use as the Windows or Macintosh system it runs on
- IP-GOLD works with all the popular standards – Email, WWW, Usenet News, FTP, Telnet and lots, lots more

And IP-GOLD can be yours for just £15.00 a month (plus £50 one-off joining fee). (All prices exclude VAT.)

Special offer

Around the world in eighty hours – a free demo disk giving you eighty hours free Internet access and £25 off your joining fee!

To get your free demo disk, just photocopy this page and post it to:

> **CityScape Internet Services Ltd.**
> **Alexandria House**
> **9 Covent Garden**
> **Cambridge CB1 2HR**

And don't forget to include your address!

To explore the Internet...

For a limited time only, Demon Internet Ltd offers you the opportunity to connect to the Internet for up to one month FREE!

Take the chance while you have it

THIS OFFER IS ONLY VALID UP TO AND INCLUDING 31ST DECEMBER 1995

Terms of special voucher offer

Demon Internet Ltd offer a trial connection to the Internet making use of our full services and support lines for up to one calendar month via a standard Dial Up account.

We work in calendar months so to make the best use of this offer you should apply at the start of the month. By accepting this offer you are subscribing to the service on an on-going basis until you cancel. Cancellation should be made to us in writing and if you cancel during the first month you will have paid nothing. If you carry on, as we hope you will, you will then pay the joining fee and start paying the monthly fee which is due in advance of using the service.

Joining fee £12.50 plus VAT   Monthly fee £10.00 plus VAT

There are no usage or on-line time charges. When joining you must send payment details in the form of one of the following:
1)   Credit card details (Visa or Mastercard)
2)   Post-dated cheque for £132.50 + VAT = £155.68 for the 1st of the following calendar month
3)   12 post-dated cheques. The first is for £12.50 + £10.00 + VAT and is to be made for the 1st of the following month. The 11 others should be for £10.00 + VAT = £11.75 and dated the 1st of each of the subsequent months.

In any event you will not be paying for the first month.

We regret that no other forms of payment are acceptable. Accounts are deemed to be annual but you may pay monthly as described above. We do not issue VAT receipts for monthly accounts and businesses are therefore advised to join annually.

We regret that we cannot accept vouchers that do not enclose payment and these may be returned or destroyed.   *See overleaf for full ordering details*

All you need to know about the Internet **.net**

Please read carefully
In order to get connected to the Internet for one month FREE, starting on the first day of any calendar month, fill out this order coupon indicating how you would like to pay for continued Demon Internet Service. If you decide to stay connected to the Internet after your month's free access you will be charged a connection fee (see details of charges below). If you decide NOT to remain connected to the Internet, you MUST inform Demon Internet Ltd, in writing, before the end of the month. This will prevent you from being charged the connection fee. Please not that withou receipt of either a cheque or credit card information you will NOT be connected for this trial offer.

Charges if you stay connected:

By credit card (Mastercard, Visa…) £12.50 + VAT joining fee, plus £10 + VAT monthly charge.

By cheque (cheques should be post-dated, for the first day of a calendar month and MUST be submitted with this offer) £155.68 (includes 12 months' connection, £12.50 joining fee, and VAT)

If you have submitted a cheque, and you decide not to continue with your Demon account, it will be returned to you if you have included an SAE, otherwise it will be destroyed. VAT receipts can only be issued for people paying annually.

Your name (full name please) ....

Company name (if applicable)...

Address ....

....Business Tel No: ....Home Tel No: ....

Credit Card No:.................................Expiry Date ....Monthly or Annual account? ....
(if paying by Mastercard or Visa)

Credit Card address (if different to above): ....

....

Machine name 1st choice_____demon.co.uk 4 to 8 characters

Machine name 2nd choice _____demon.co.uk 4 to 8 characters

Signed ....Date..

Please complete this orginal voucher only (photocopies are not acceptable) and post to:
Demon Internet Ltd, 42 Hendon Lane, Finchley, London N3 1TT
Cheques should be made payable to Demon Internet Ltd. Tel: 0181 349 0063

the internet magazine
.net All you need to know about the Internet

.net magazine
subscription offer

Save £5.50 and receive three trial issues! The normal subscription rate for .net magazine is £35.40, but readers of this book can subscribe at the special rate of £29.90!

If you are not fully satisfied after you've received these three trial issues you are entitled to a full money-back refund.

.net is your monthly guide to the Internet, helping you to make sense of the jargon and guiding you to the best that the Net has to offer. Whether you're looking for something new or weird, for leisure or business, .net magazine will take you there.

Regular "How-to" guides combine with in-depth features every month to give you the chance to thoroughly explore the Net without the trouble or trauma normally associated with going on-line.

Take out a no-risk subscription to .net magazine NOW.

Subscribe now and you'll **SAVE** over **£5 OFF** the price that you'd normally pay at the newsagents and get every issue delivered direct to your home. We're sure that you'll love .net so we're happy to give you a no-risk guarantee: If you are in any way unhappy with .net then you can cancel your subscription at any time and receive a full refund. Complete and return the subscription form right away or

telephone: 01225 822511 or
e-mail: subs@futurenet.co.uk

(See overleaf for subscription order form)

All you need to know about the Internet **.net**

Subscription order form

the internet magazine
.net

Yes, please accept my subscription to .net magazine at a **saving** of **£5.50**. I understand that I may cancel my subscription if not fully satisfied after receiving my first three issues for a full money-back refund*.

(*This offer is available to UK residents only. Overseas rates are available on application. Please note the deadline for cancellation is one week after receipt of your third issue.)

Title (Mr/Mrs/Miss) _____Initials_____Surname_____

Address _____

_____Postcode_____

Method of payment (please tick one):

☐ Access   ☐ Visa   ☐ Cheque   ☐ Postal order

Credit card no _____

Expiry date _____

Signature _____Date _____

☐ Tick here if you do not wish to receive details of future **.net** products.

Send this form to **.net Subscriptions, Future Publishing Ltd, FREEPOST (BS4900), Somerton, Somerset TA11 6BR**

the internet magazine
.net All you need to know about the Internet   FBB 0647